# Estate
# Jewelry
## 1760 to 1960

### Diana Sanders Cinamon

Schiffer Publishing Ltd

4880 Lower Valley Road  Atglen, PA 19310

# Dedication

This book is dedicated to the loving memory of
Pearl Rodman
who accepted me into her family and her heart;
and to my husband and partner, Seth,
who took on a thousand tasks so I could focus on one.

Designed by John P. Cheek
Cover design by Bruce Waters
Type set in Didi/Lydian BT

ISBN: 978-0-7643-3300-2
Printed in China

Schiffer Books are available at special discounts for bulk purchases for sales promotions or premiums. Special editions, including personalized covers, corporate imprints, and excerpts can be created in large quantities for special needs. For more information contact the publisher:

Published by Schiffer Publishing Ltd.
4880 Lower Valley Road
Atglen, PA 19310
Phone: (610) 593-1777; Fax: (610) 593-2002
E-mail: Info@schifferbooks.com

For the largest selection of fine reference books on this and related subjects, please visit our web site at www.schifferbooks.com
We are always looking for people to write books on new and related subjects. If you have an idea for a book please contact us at the above address.

This book may be purchased from the publisher.
Include $5.00 for shipping.
Please try your bookstore first.
You may write for a free catalog.

In Europe, Schiffer books are distributed by
Bushwood Books
6 Marksbury Ave.
Kew Gardens
Surrey TW9 4JF England
Phone: 44 (0) 20 8392 8585; Fax: 44 (0) 20 8392 9876
E-mail: info@bushwoodbooks.co.uk
Website: www.bushwoodbooks.co.uk

# Contents

# Acknowledgments

Although my education and teaching experience in this specific subject spans a decade, this is a first attempt at writing a jewelry book. Most would agree that a contributor would be happy to have their name appear in the acknowledgment pages of a book by Dorothy Rainwater or Vivienne Becker. As a relatively unknown author it is then a more difficult task to rally support for a project like this. So first and foremost thanks go out to Lothar Vallot, chair of the gemology department at Santiago Canyon College in Orange, California. Many of the contributors are members of our alumni association who responded to the notices Lothar sent out in support of this project. More than one person confessed that had it not been for his endorsement, they would not have come forward to offer their support.

Special thanks to Diana Miller, not only for allowing me to photograph her collection, but also for her continued support throughout our professional careers as appraisers.

Special thanks and acknowledgments to Heather Gates, my best friend "ever since we could wear bikinis". Together we have braved classes, seminars, flea markets, antique malls, estate sales, museums, and the rigors of Lothar's infamous colored gemstones class.

Thanks to my mother, Giorgina for encouraging conversations and warm meals after many long day's work and travel to complete this project; and thanks for just being my mom.

In early conversations with Nancy Schiffer, my editor, she said, "We all stand on other people's shoulders." While this book contains much information not found in contemporary sources, the foundation for this book comes from other authors and other teachers, such as my colleague, Christie Romero, and notable author and speaker, C. Jeanenne Bell.

The challenging part about putting a book together with a price guide is the sheer volume of jewelry required to make it comprehensive. Accomplishing that takes collectors, each with their own areas of interest. To Lisa Olson, Roberta Knauer Mullings, Debbie White, Cristina Romeo (my sister), Joy Ste. Marie, Jodi Lenocker, Ebert and Company, Sabrina Chapman, Agave House, Mildred Iacovetti, Navon Vance, Barbara Seman, Kitty Barrett, Bélen Córdova and Cathleen Peel: thank you for opening your homes and sharing your passion for collecting.

# Introduction

My first job after college was selling wine to retailers and restaurateurs. Aside from developing the ability to distinguish vintage years blindfolded, I learned something very important about the price of a bottle of wine: Do not expect the same thing from a bottle of wine for which you paid $20 as you would from one that you paid $200. In fact, when wines are judged in contests, they are judged for their quality within a given price range.

Let's apply the same rule to jewelry, comparing Bakelite to Bakelite, not Bakelite to Persian turquoise. One may always be quaint and the other sublime, but both have their place in history and in this book. Both have value to their respective collectors.

It is important to learn to tell the difference between materials like Bakelite and turquoise because material content does affect value. There are two chapters devoted to basic identification techniques for gem materials, metals, and jewelry fittings and findings. While reading this book is not intended to be a substitute for gemology courses, it provides a foundation for distinguishing materials used in antique and vintage jewelry. In either case, learning takes practice; so take the time to perfect your identification techniques. Look at jewelry, handle jewelry, and always carry a 10-power, fully corrected loupe, a magnet, a black light, and a penlight.

An important goal for this book was its organization. Every chapter on periods and styles is organized the same way: history behind the fashion, fashion affecting jewelry styles, jewelry styles, specific types of jewelry worn, and popular materials and techniques of the period. There is a style timeline at the conclusion of Chapter 7 that summarizes the dates for each style, showing how various styles overlapped. Understanding periods and styles is a powerful tool when coupled with the identification sections that follow.

All the jewelry in chapter 11, the price guide, is listed by form first, then by time period. Therefore, bracelets are together chronologically and necklaces are together chronologically, etc. The identification chapters are together. Wherever practical, jewelry was photographed to show the fittings and findings rather than describe them in the captions. Repairs, alterations, and general condition issues that affect value are noted in the captions. Condition is extremely important in jewelry. Damage or repairs to the front of a piece are far more critical than damage or repairs to the back, although the collector should always strive to purchase undamaged pieces.

The bibliography contains primarily 20th century references. Many of the illustrations are from 19th century catalogs, magazines, and books, and their sources are sited in the chapter where they are referenced. Where practical, the prices have been left on period catalog pages. Even the novice can see that the most humble pieces of jewelry are worth many times more than originally advertised. Hopefully, this book will give you the confidence to buy them when you find them.

# SECTION ONE

# Chapter 1
# Late Georgian Jewelry
## 1760 to 1837

## Historical Background

The events and stylistic preferences leading up to the late Georgian period, both directly and indirectly, influenced late Georgian jewelry styles. As had been the custom in past times, nobility and the wealthy were the dominant influences on fashion. If there was one country that can be said to have lead fashion most often, it was France. Louis XIV, ruled France from 1643 until 1715. Nicknamed the Sun King, Louis gave elaborate parties at his palace at Versailles. These affairs were held outdoors, during the day. Sometime during his reign, a transition began featuring evening, indoor parties lit by candlelight.

This not only affected the type of jewelry that was worn, but also began a distinction between daytime jewelry and evening jewelry. Diamonds sparkled more by candlelight and were the preferred gemstone for evening jewelry. This trend in the distinction between day and evening jewelry continued to guide styles for the rest of the century and into the next.

Jewelry styles in the late Georgian period reflected the lingering tastes for the Rococo style. A prominent feature of Rococo was the preference for delicate, all-over patterning of foliage like acanthus leaves, and where practical, asymmetrical designs.

Sometime around 1755, a new style, called Neo-Classical, began to influence the decorative arts, including jewelry. Inspired by the excavations of ancient ruins in Italy and Greece, some of the style elements include Prince-of-Wales feathers, Greek key patterns, mythological figures, braziers (torches), and attributes of music. Marie Antoinette (wife of Louis XVI and Queen of France) had as her personal device, two turtledoves above two hymeneal (marriage) torches.

The influence of the French in decorative art stops abruptly with the French Revolution beginning in 1789. The leaders of the subsequent "Reign of Terror" abolished the system of guilds that included French jewelers. Aristocracy either fled the country or had their heads chopped off by guillotines that worked relentlessly since the execution of Louis XVI and Marie Antoinette.

It is at this time that fashion influences shift to other countries such as Great Britain, Germany, Italy, and Russia. There are some unique jewelry styles, like sentimental jewelry and hair jewelry that are directly inspired by British romanticism.

While the United States was still a young country, America had been colonized since the early 17th century. By the late 18th century there was a substantial jewelry and fancy goods industry in the United States. Most people are aware that Paul Revere was a silversmith, but few people realize that he did make jewelry and that a few examples of rings survive and are attributed to his workmanship; but in general, American jewelry styles followed more conservative fashions like those in Great Britain.

As European monarchies suffered the direct and indirect consequences of uprisings and revolts, the Georgian era also saw the dawn of the *Industrial* Revolution. While sources disagree as to exactly when the Industrial Revolution began, it is generally accepted as beginning in the mid- to late 18th century with the impact of rapidly changing technology felt throughout the 19th century, many of which directly affect the manufacture of jewelry.

As the 18th century ends, France enters an era of stability under the military leadership of Napoleon Bonaparte. The French treasury is essentially depleted and Napoleon Bonaparte sets out on various campaigns to liberate countries like Germany, Belgium, the Netherlands, Spain, and Italy. Some of the effects of his campaigns can be seen in the changes Napoleon made to these countries' gold and silver marking laws. When Napoleon and his troops land in Egypt in 1799, Egyptian antiquities and relics fascinate him. At this point Egyptian motifs are added to the neo-classical style.

With Napoleon defeated in 1815, the Congress of Vienna convenes to re-draw Europe's boundaries. France's royalty are restored as rulers of the country. During this short period of peace, we again see the French influence in fashion, with many of the jewelers returning to design jewelry for their former clients. The look is much more simple as returning aristocracy have lost much of their wealth. This simple and more delicate look is reflected in the jewelry proportions of the early 19th century.

A final influence on fashion comes with the development of machine made paper and improvements in the printing press, making literature accessible to the average man. A popular novel *The History of the Renowned Prince Arthur, King of Britain*, written by Thomas Malory in 1816, fuels romanticism, a revival of the age of chivalry, and sets the stage for the Gothic Revival motifs that are very popular by 1825. More importantly, magazines like *La Belle Assemblée* make it possible for ladies of all classes to follow fashion trends.

# Late Georgian Fashion Influences

Up until the French Revolution, bodices were tight and low cut with a large stiff, v-shaped panel in the front to hold the breasts in place. Jewelry complimented the cut of the dress more than the style of the dress. When stiff, v-shaped bodices were popular in the mid to late 18th century, large v-shaped bodice ornaments called stomachers and bow-brooches went well with the clothing weight and proportions. Brocade fabrics were well accented with floral-spray brooches. The width of the dress looked balanced with large, wide earrings, like the girandole style.

**Stomacher** exhibited at the Great Exhibition of 1851.

**Bow brooch** exhibited at the Great Exhibition of 1851.

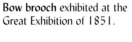
AH! QUELLE ANTIQUITÉ !!!

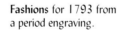
**Fashions** for 1793 from a period engraving.

Styles change dramatically from 1760 to 1790 as shown by two period engravings from 1793. The couple on the left is dressed in current fashions as they point to the outdated couple on the right dressed in fashions from 1778. The change occurs in just fifteen years. The impact of the neo-classical style led the fashion industry to copy the look of ancient Greek and Roman clothes.

When these light and filmy, neo-classical dresses became popular, traditional jewelry forms were no longer wearable. Instead, long chains, very long earrings, and multi-strand chokers suited these new dress styles. Short puffy sleeves allowed women to wear bracelets on their upper arms. Even the weight of the jewelry tended to be lighter. 18th century staples like large girandole earrings do not work well with light muslin fabrics.

**Comparison of Fashions** from 1768.

The waistline continues to rise to directly under the bust line just after 1800. The trend towards what we today call an *empire waistline* continues into the 19th century until about 1825 when the waistline drops to just below the ribcage. The skirt is at this point is somewhat funnel-shaped.

*Evening Dresses*

**1802 fashions** from *La Belle Assemblee*.

**1825 fashions** from *La Belle Assemblee*. Lady with a van dyke collar wears a sautoir with a lorgnette and cuff bracelets.

In keeping with the numerous decorative arts revivals that occur in the 19th century, women's clothing designers include specific elements such as a *van dyke* collar, a bodice *a la Sévigné*, dresses with Egyptian borders, or embroidered Greek fret designs with numerous variations. The fabrics are heavier; the sleeves are longer.

By 1827 the shoulders begin to widen. The skirts are still basically funnel-shaped, but ruffles and rolls of fabric have been added to the hemline. The overall look begins to look more hourglass shaped. These heavier fabrics could once again support the weighty look of large belt buckles.

1827 evening fashions from *La Belle Assemblee*. Ladies wear pendant earrings, double strand and festoon necklaces, and cuff bracelets. Lady on the left wears a bodice *a la Sevigné*.

1827 daytime fashions from *La Belle Assemblee*. Ladies wear sautoirs, one lady wears a large belt buckle.

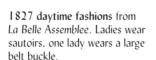

In 1828, the waistline has returned to its natural position. Shoulders are wide and sleeves beneath them become voluminous. Skirts are widening, taking on more of a bell-shape. The weight of the jewelry increases with double strands, and festoons to balance the new sizes of the shoulders, arms and skirts.

By the end of the Georgian era, the bodice and the upper portion of the sleeves are cut from one piece. The lower portion of the sleeves become more bell-shaped, and in a more conservative Victorian era, the bust is covered, even for eveningwear.

Another significant trend that affected jewelry is hats. Throughout the late Georgian era, women wore hats. In the early 19th century, turbans become very popular, both of which allow for the wearing of earrings. Bonnets become more popular in the 19th century and are stylish for daytime wear. Because of the way that the bonnets covered the ears, earrings were not typically worn outdoors, during the day, but continued to be popular for indoor gatherings.

**1828 fashions** from *La Belle Assemblee* showing jewelry with heavier proportions.

**1837 fashions** from *Blackwood's Lady's Magazine*.

# Popular Jewelry Styles and Forms

### Rococo and Neo-Classical

Lingering tastes for the Rococo style persist throughout the 1760s. The most common element seen in jewelry is the bowknot, or true lover's knot, illustrated earlier. It can be seen as an unaccompanied bow, as in the case of the Sévigné brooch or as an accent to other Rococo themes.

Jewelry in the late Georgian era emphasized the gemstones, not the metal the gems were set in, with exposed metal kept to a minimum. Because of this, Rococo style elements common in other forms of decorative arts are less frequent in Rococo jewelry. One example would be the use of the cyma curve, often expressed as foliage like acanthus leaves. It can be found in chatelaines of the period, or forming the borders of lockets, pendants, and rings as in the case of the memorial brooch shown.

Asymmetry is also less frequent in Rococo jewelry. Most jewelry requires balanced weight to be wearable. Asymmetry does occur in the brooches and aigrettes, both of which can be pinned or fastened into place.

Late Georgian sentimental brooch with border of cyma curves and a later addition of a chain safety.

Neoclassical themes were abundant in late Georgian jewelry. Stars, trophy motifs, mythological figures, and laurel wreaths were all popular jewelry themes. Cameos and intaglios probably lead the list of popular jewelry motifs, reaching their height of popularity in the early 19th century (Intaglios cut into the surface, instead of standing above it.) Women wore several cameos at the same time. They wore suites of jewelry set with multiple cameos. Empress Josephine owned a shell cameo diadem and a parurer set with intaglio carnelians. In addition to shells and gem materials like agate and cornelian, cameos were made of ceramics, micromosaics, pietra dura, and colored glass.

### Sentimental and Memorial Jewelry

Although the two dominant styles are Rococo and Neo-classical, there were sub-styles that occur in jewelry that are not seen in other forms of decorative arts. Sentimental and memorial jewelry were two sub-styles that took on a wide variety of expressions.

Memorial jewelry, in particular, began to regain popularity around 1742 when a popular English novel was published that talked about life, death, and immortality. Both memorial jewelry and sentimental jewelry could be expressed in the form a portrait miniature, hair jewelry, serpent motifs, acrostics, or posies. Examples using a combination of elements were also made.

### Portraits

Miniature portraits painted on porcelain plaques or enameled plaques could be mounted in brooches, lockets or rings. All forms are very popular in the late 18th century and early 19th century. One shown here is a portrait of the Empress Josephine wearing a portrait brooch, presumably of Napoleon.

A special kind of portrait jewelry involved having a painted portrait of a lover's eye and eyebrow. There are conflicting stories as to the origin of the eye jewelry, but one source shows the style originating in Paris and made popular in England by Prince George when he secretly wed a Catholic widow. They exchanged portraits of each other's eyes. There may be examples as far back as 1790. They continue in popularity until the 1820s.

19th century engraving of Empress Josephine wearing a portrait locket.

## Hair

Remembrances of loved ones took other forms in the late Georgian era. Rings, brooches and lockets were made using human hair. The most common form that survives uses a locket of human hair plaited and set under a piece of rock quartz, usually bordered with garnets, seed pearls, or enameling. They are typically quite small, measuring only about an inch across, generally becoming larger (up to two inches) in the early 19th century.

Another type of hair jewelry involved using the hair to create a pigment that was then painted on ivory. A common theme depicts a women standing by a memorial monument that stands under a weeping willow. Others may show just an urn beneath a weeping willow. Sometimes the scene incorporated the actual strands of hair. It was also common to have names, initials, and dates either engraved or as part of the design. Shapes tended to be oval, navette, or rounded rectangles as shown in examples of this period.

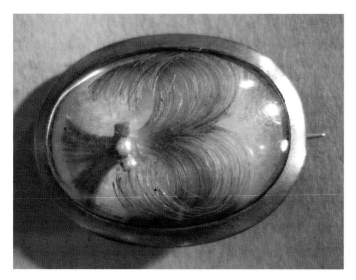

Early 19th century brooch with hair and seed pearls

## Serpents

Another popular sentimental theme was that of a serpent biting his tail, a symbol of eternity. Sometimes the serpent encircled a central lock of plaited hair set under clear quartz. Serpents continued to be popular for most of the 19th century.

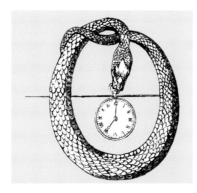

Engraving of a serpent watch pin from the Great Exhibition of 1851.

## Acrostics and Posies

Even Napoleon Bonaparte fell under the romantic spell of sentimental jewelry. He had a bracelet made for the birth of his niece where the first initial of each gem spelled out her first name. These acrostics took more generic forms as the 19th century progressed, usually spelling out the word "dearest" or "regard". The French used the words "Amitie" and "Souvenir".

Posy rings were engraved with a short phrase or motto. Their use dates to antiquity, but in the late 18th century they are especially common on wedding rings with short sayings like "love and obaye" or "fear God and love me".

## Floral and Naturalistic Motifs

By the 1760s naturalism returns to jewelry motifs, most often expressed by floral bouquets and baskets of flowers. By now, the preference for color returns with floral sprays richly accented with colored gemstones and delicate enameling. Brooches featured diamonds and colored gemstones, often tied with a true lover's knot. Rings were made in the form of floral baskets called "giardinetti", an Italian word that means "little garden".

## Gothic Revival

Quatrefoils, rosettes, lancet arches, shields, linen fold, and tracery all resembling the cathedrals from which they drew their inspiration, the Gothic jewelry style can be seen as early as 1825 and continues to be popular until about 1870. Our example dates to the early Victorian era.

19th century Gothic Revival brooch in the shape of a quatrefoil. (Collection of Heather Gates)

## Late Georgian Jewelry

In many ways, jewelry of the 1760s and 1770s was a continuation of earlier styles and forms. Bodice ornaments like the *Sévigné* or bow-brooch were made popular by the Marquise de Sévigné in the 17th century and remained a jewelry staple until changes in clothing fashions made them impractical to wear.

Another style of brooch was made in the shape of a small bouquet, or floral spray. They were asymmetrical in form and very natural looking. Early in the century, they were made with few exceptions of pavé-set diamonds, paste, or some other colorless gemstone until colored gemstones become popular again around 1760. One shown is a portrait of Madame Juno wearing both a floral spray brooch.

*Stomachers* were another type of bodice ornament. They were often sewn directly onto the bodice of the dress. When worn with brocade fabrics, stomachers and brooches added glittering highlights to the fabric.

19th century engraving of a portrait of Madame Junot wearing a floral spray brooch.

Large earrings were made *à la girandole* (like a branched candlestick or wall sconce with drops). They were usually made with one large round gem or cluster of gems with three drops (usually pear-shaped) below them. If the earrings had just one drop, they were referred to as *pendeloque*. The example shown is a pair of late Georgian girandole style earrings.

Pendeloque earrings were worn in the mid 1700s, but become more popular and generally replace girandole earrings towards the end of the 18th century. The Pendeloque becomes longer and thinner in the late 18th century, to match the long drape of the dresses. The engraving shows the Empress Josephine wearing a pair of pendeloque earrings.

JOSEPHINE
Painting by Gèrard

19th century engraving of Empress Josephine wearing a tiara and pendeloque earrings.

Late Georgian girandole earrings, mine-cut diamonds set in silver. (Courtesy of Lisa L. Olson)

Another type of earrings called *poissardes* were elongated hoop earrings. The hoop could be set with a central gemstone, a vertical row of gemstones or some other decorative element. They have a unique side view. The hoop is held in place by an s-shaped support visible from the side. Poissardes are illustrated in chapter 9.

Necklaces were usually made as a single row of cluster-set gems until the last quarter of the 18th century when the *rivière* style became popular. The rivière style featured a single row of individually set, graduated gemstones. Necklaces become heavier through the 1820s with double rows and festoons adding weight. The 1827 fashion plate shows a woman wearing a double strand necklace; the other wears a festoon style.

Another type of necklace, called a *sautoir* becomes a popular compliment to the Neo-classical dress. At this time, they are long, fine chains, or rows of chains. They were originally worn over one shoulder and under the other, but by the 19th century, they were worn like long necklaces, typically holding an eyeglass at the end. The woman shown in the 1825 fahion plate is holding the eyeglass attached to her sautoir. Other types of sautoirs had serpent motifs. By 1825 the sautoir has acquired a slide.

In the 1820s, Fortunato Pio Castellani was involved with excavating numerous Etruscan burial sites in Italy. One type of necklace, the fringe necklace was inspired by Castellani's excavations and replicated by him. A portrait in the Guggenheim Museum shows the young Countess Samoilova some time around 1832, wearing a fringe necklace. Hers was made of metal; other surviving fringe necklaces were made with coral, amber, garnet, and other semi-precious gemstones.

Simple bead or pearl chokers are worn throughout the late Georgian era, but the proportions change with the weight and style of the clothing. Sometimes, women wore lace or ribbon chokers, attaching a brooch to complete the look. Chokers went well with the Neo-classical styles. Around 1806, multi-strand, lightweight chains called *jasseron* were worn.

*Tiaras, and aigrettes* were worn in the hair. The tiara was a semi-circular band that rested on the forehead and was fastened into the hair. Reflecting the Neo-classical styles, they became popular in the early 19th century. The aigrette was another piece of jewelry made to be worn in the hair, although they were worn earlier in the 18th century. Very few aigrettes survived the Georgian era. Typically taking on Rococo, asymmetrical proportions, they often took the form of feathers or floral sprays. The image shown is a late Georgian aigrette that was later converted to a brooch. Tiaras and aigrettes were considered appropriate for eveningwear.

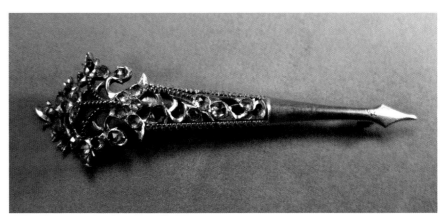

**Late Georgian aigrette**, later conversion to a brooch. (Courtesy of finderskeepersvintage.com)

*Ferronnières* were also worn in the hair. They became popular around 1824. The ferronnière was a delicate chain that fit across the forehead and featured a central accent like a gem or cluster of gems. They continued to be popular into the early Victorian era. The image shows a fashion plate from 1835 with the woman in the center wearing a ferronnière. The inspiration for the ferronnière comes from a portrait attributed to Leonardo da Vince. The woman in that portrait wears a chain across her forehead set with a central jewel. Ferronnières were acceptable for daytime wear.

Bracelets were made to match other pieces of jewelry, like brooches, necklaces or earrings; they were usually made then as single rows of cluster-set gems or paste. They fit tightly. In the late 18th century women also wore matching bracelets on their upper arms.

Cuff bracelets are commonly worn in pairs on the wrist by the early 19th century and usually featured a central ornament, or central cluster setting.

Buckles were another popular form of jewelry. By 1730 women wore them with ribbons for chokers, bracelets, and belts, and were initially very small. They become fashionable for men by about 1740. Men wore them to fasten their shoes and knee bands instead of using ribbons. For men, the metal and gem content was an indication of status. Or a man might wear cut-steel buckles during the week, and wear silver buckles to church on Sunday. In general, buckles are very popular until about 1790, when neo-classical styles made them unfashionable for women's jewelry. Buckles were considered to be daytime jewelry for both men and women.

Rings date to antiquity, although some styles like sentimental or memorial rings, originate in the late Georgian era. Sentimental motifs could be love tokens or in remembrance of a deceased loved one. They survive in large quantities compared

1835 fashion engraving with woman in the center wearing a ferronnière.

to other forms and styles of jewelry. As remembrances, they would not have been melted down and remade into more stylish pieces, as was most other precious jewelry of the period. Wedding bands are also worn. Many rings of this era have dates and inscriptions, making them easy to date and attribute. Rings were popular for both men and women. They were made in both precious and semi-precious gemstones. Cameo rings become popular with the rise in popularity of the neo-classical styles.

The *Chatelaine* was an important piece of jewelry. The wristwatch had not been invented, so those women who owned watches, wore them on elaborate chains called *equipage*. A hook plate slipped over the belt with either chains or hinged panels hanging from the hook plate. The watch and other "necessaries" like keys, hung from the chatelaine. Chatelaines were worn during the daytime.

In the 18th century suites of jewelry were called *parurers*. Although not a strict definition, a parurer is five or more matching pieces of jewelry. Sometimes parurers were made with additional pendeloques that could be added to pieces of jewelry as the wearer saw fit.

# Popular Gems and Gem Materials

One of the most noticeable changes in late Georgian jewelry occurs in the use of color. By 1760, fashion influences had grown tired of colorless gemstones. We begin to see more colored enamels and colored gemstones accentuating diamonds and it's imitators but diamonds continued to be set without color until about 1770.

Diamond and colored gemstones were sometimes enhanced. Frederick Strass a French jeweler developed a method to add colored foil backing to diamonds around 1734. Other gemstones were commonly foil-backed to improve their color.

Those who could not afford diamonds wore "paste", a high lead content glass cut into various gem shapes since the late 17th century. Strass improved upon the original English paste formula. Strass was marketing his flint glass gems by 1734. Paste or *false-stone work* or as it was also called, was well accepted in Europe by the mid 18th century. Diamonds were not the only gemstones that were made in paste. Some of the more creative materials were an opal paste, a kind of pink milk glass, and blue-based aventurine paste with gold flecks. The image is a small paste brooch set in silver, dating between 1800 and 1825.

Late Georgian floral spray brooch in cut-steel, front and back views.

Late Georgian paste brooch, set in silver, 1800 to 1825. (Author's collection)

Marcasites and cut-steel and were also popular materials to imitate diamonds. Marcasites, sometimes called *fool's gold*, are actually faceted iron pyrites. They were usually set like gemstones. Earlier in the century marcasites were considered to be a material for dandies, but gained acceptability in the late 18th century.

Cut-steel looks a lot like marcasite from the top, but cut-steel is actually made like a tiny nail with the shaft riveted to the jewelry. This distinction makes it easy to tell the difference between the two. Since cut-steel was very labor intensive and expensive to make, it was an acceptable jewelry material for the wealthy. Mathew Bolton set up a factory in 1762 to make cut-steel jewelry. In 1775 Bolton teamed up with Josiah Wedgwood to make jasperware cameos accented and trimmed with cut-steel. In 1780 an Englishman took the process to France and began making cut-steel jewelry. Even Marie Antoinette had jewelry made of cut-steel. The front and back of a late Georgian cut-steel brooch are shown.

Natural pearls were always in demand with imitations made since the 16th century. One popular method of making artificial pearls was to coat the *inside* of a glass bead.

With the restoration of the Bourbons to France in 1814, few could afford diamonds. Most of them wore paste and semi-precious gemstones for evening wear. Neo-classical clothing did not feature colored brocade fabrics so this addition of color did much to liven up the evening toilette. Yellow topaz and amethyst were favored, but aquamarine and turquoise were also popular.

From 1770 to about 1790, Russian state jewels for daytime use included agates, garnets, river pearls, and other semi-precious gemstones. In the low countries, (the Netherlands, Belgium, and the German states), amber and silver were considered appropriate for daytime wear.

Around 1800, moss agate, carnelian, onyx, and seed pearls are added to the list of popular gem materials for daytime wear.

Both Micromosaic jewelry and pietra dura jewelry also became a popular jewelry purchase for those taking the Grand Tour through Florence and Rome in the late 18th and 19th century, and are considered to be Neo-classical in inspiration. Micromosaic jewelry was made of tiny glass rods that were fitted into a frame with mastic to hold the pieces in place. The Vatican produced them commercially since 1727, but romantic scenes date to the 19th century. Pietra Dura cameos are made of hard stone material like marble and agate. Larger pieces are cut out and fit together, much like the interlocking pieces of a jigsaw puzzle to form a portrait or scene. Examples of both micromosaics and pietra dura can be found in price guide section.

Piqué was a technique originally used for necessaries, etuis, and trinket boxes but became popular for use in jewelry around 1800. Typically using the shell of the hawksbill tortoise, tiny pieces of gold, silver, or brass were inlayed into the heated shell. Piqué continued to be popular throughout the 19th century. Chapter 8 has identification pointers for tortoise.

# Decorating, Finishing, and Other Techniques

There is a noticeable transition from the late 18th century to the early 19th century in the overall construction of jewelry. Gems set with open backs, or à jour, now replaced the delicate pavé-set and bead-set jewels, which previously replaced the cluster setting.

In the early 19th century, returning French aristocracy has little money to spend on jewelry. As a result, *cannetille*, a course form of filigree was a popular way to make a little gold and silver go a long way. It can be coarsely made, but some surviving examples are beautifully executed.

*Jasseron*, a very fine chain worn in multiples, was another technique that created the illusion of weight. Paris jewelers also began setting diamonds in spreading collets, which made the diamonds look larger. The image shows a portrait of Madame Riviere in a portrait by Ingres wearing a jasseron necklace.

Another decorative metal technique originated in Prussia (now Germany). The Royal Prussian Foundry opened in 1804, producing an early form of *Berlin Iron* jewelry. Featuring delicately cast designs, it was very popular well into the early Victorian era. When Napoleon captured Berlin in 1806, he had the molds transferred to Paris. By 1815 there was no distinguishable difference between the jewelry made in Berlin and Paris.

It was also common to set colorless gemstones like diamonds or white topaz, in silver with gold used to accent colored gemstones.

The jewelry industry does not escape the effects of the Industrial Revolution. By 1817, rolled gold, a heat-fused sheet metal featuring a gold top and bottom with a base metal center, was used to decrease the amount of gold used in jewelry. Another innovation was the use of machine, die-stamped jewelry. By 1820, machine-stamped designs are common.

**Late Georgian brooch/pendant**, cannetille, topaz, and seed pearl. (Courtesy of Roberta Knauer Mullings, G.G.)

**Engraving** from a portrait of Madame Riviére, wearing a jasseron necklace.

Since gold and silver were scarce, Christopher Pinchbeck found a way to eliminate it entirely. He introduced his brass alloy called pinchbeck. It was an excellent substitute for gold, and in common use by 1820.

Several forms of enameling were also popular in the late Georgian era, *Bilston enameling*, *Limoges enameling*, and *Grisaille enameling*. All three techniques involve painting on a flat surface with repeated applications and firings to finish the piece. The French excelled at this process. Well-executed examples are typically attributed to Limoges although the Venetians were also known for painted enamel jewelry. Bilston enameling designs tends to be less finely executed, with factories active in England from 1749 to 1831. Grisaille is a form of painted enamel done in two colors, such as black and white or blue and white. Sentimental jewelry using hair pigment to paint on ivory is considered to be a form of grisaille, although not an enameling technique. An image here shows an Early Victorian locket executed in grisaille enameling.

*Champlevé* enameling was used to accent jewelry like floral sprays when color became popular again, although in Spain, the preference for this type of enameling was never entirely abandoned. Unsigned, enameled jewelry that dates to the early 18th century is typically attributed to Spanish origins.

**Early 19th century locket** with Grisaille enameling. (Courtesy of Cathleen L. Peel)

## Chapter 2
# Early Victorian Jewelry
### 1837 to 1860

## Historical Background

By the time Victoria becomes Queen of England in 1837, the industrial revolution is strongly underway, changing in particular the way jewelry is made. Many mass-production methods have been introduced, making jewelry more affordable for a developing middle class. This was the start of a Romantic Period in jewelry design.

Now that the Napoleonic wars have ended, safe travel becomes possible again. The world's first mass transit system, the railroad, is well established by 1837, both in the United States and England. Italy, Switzerland, and France follow closely behind making international travel and touring a possibility for an emerging middle class with money to spend.

*The Grand Tour,* once a travel itinerary for elite young men, now becomes a favorite venue for this new group of travelers, who now bring their wives and young daughters for their cultural education. The Grand Tour typically left from Dover traveling across the English Channel to Calais, then through Paris to Rome, and finishing with Pompeii and Herculaneum. With each stop, the natural choice of souvenirs for women was jewelry.

Like most young women of her time Queen Victoria was also fond of jewelry. When she gave gifts, it was frequently jewelry. Just 18 years old when she became Queen of England, Victoria was soon urged to marry. Having a choice of two young men, Victoria proposed to Albert, her German cousin, in 1839. They were very much in love, a fortunate coincidence for royals who were expected to marry for political reasons. Albert gave Victoria a betrothal ring in the form of a serpent, a sign of eternity, sparking a renewed interest in both romanticism and serpent jewelry.

Victoria and Albert wed in 1840. They were devoted to each other, and although Prince Albert was supportive, suggestive, and helpful, Victoria was queen. Wanting very much to make a real contribution, Albert came up with the idea to hold an international exhibition that would feature the progress made by the on-going industrial revolution and in 1851, the Great Exhibition opened in Hyde Park.

Aside from being a financial success, it gave the world an opportunity to see the wonders of commerce from participating countries around the globe. The profits were used to establish museums for public benefit and education. In addition to having access to exhibits of the world's commerce, the average citizen would, in the years to come, have access to exhibits of the world's art, including medieval and renaissance jewelry, and jewelry designs.

Thomas Cook also wanted to bring education to the working class, believing that this new middleclass should spend less time drinking and more time in pursuit of higher education. He organized "Cook's Conducted Tours" bringing travelers to the Great Exhibition in 1851. In 1855 when France hosted the Paris Exposition, Thomas Cook offered travel itineraries from Dover to Calais and through Dieppe, a center for ivory carving in France. After stopping to buy souvenirs (and ivory jewelry), the tour went on the Exposition.

There were two dominant themes at the Paris exposition, Gothic Revival and Rococo Revival. Queen Victoria preferred the romanticism associated with the Gothic age of chivalry. Queen Victoria was so taken with Gothic themes that she and Prince Albert had a Gothic castle built in Scotland called Balmoral. They both loved the Scottish countryside and when the state ball was held for the opening of the Great Exhibition, guests were asked to wear tartans, with Scottish agate jewelry, of course.

Across the ocean in France, Empress Eugenie sought to revive the Rococo style associated with the last period of opulence in France. Both styles enjoyed popularity in the early Victorian era. But there were sub-styles, too. Ongoing excavations in Pompeii, Crete, Rhodes, Cerveteri, Priam, and Assyria served to extend the popularity of the Neo-Classical style and its motifs in jewelry.

Now that mass-production techniques made jewelry more affordable for the average woman, it was also possible for manufacturers to market more whimsical types of jewelry, some with fleeting popularity and some that endured.

# Early Victorian Fashion Influences

Magazines like Godey's Magazine, were marketed exclusively to women, giving etiquette tips, recipes, needlework patterns, romantic stories, and fashion advice. Many of them included hand-colored fashion plates. The introduction of the lock-stitch sewing machine in 1832, gave women an opportunity to copy these fashions quickly.

Women's dresses were still made with the bust line and waist tightly corseted, the front ending in a deep v-shape. The upper portion of the sleeve is still part of the bodice, restricting a woman's arm movement. It is referred to as a drop sleeve. The size of the sleeve is more proportional to the bodice. Women wore three-quarter length, bell-shaped sleeves or long sleeves and high necklines during the day, even in the summertime.

For evening the bodice *a la Sévigné* is still popular but covers a larger area of the torso. This will accommodate larger brooches than previously worn. Most evening dresses feature three-quarter length, bell-shaped sleeves or short sleeves.

Given the ability to make clothing more quickly, it should not be a surprise that ladies skirts continue to widen, although they do not reach their fullest point until the mid-Victorian era. This "proper fullness" was initially accomplished by the use of 20 to 40 crinoline petticoats. It is not until the introduction of the hoop skirt in the late 1850s that women have some relief from the weight of up to 40 layers of fabric.

As the skirts widen, the jewelry gets larger, displaying a gradual increase over late Georgian brooches, many of which were barely an inch across.

Bonnets gain more popularity during this period. As in the late Georgian era, they do cover the ears, which made wearing earrings outdoors impractical. Hair was neatly parted in the middle and covered the ears. The example shows day and evening fashions for 1855.

1855 fashions from *The Ladies Companion*; evening attire (left), daytime attire (right).

# Popular Jewelry Styles and Forms

## Gothic Revival

The Gothic Revival style that began in the last part of the late Georgian era, is now one of two dominant styles of the early Victorian era. Aside from decorative elements like quatrefoils, rosettes, and tracery, the Gothic style also serves to renew interest in sentimental jewelry, since its inspiration comes from novels that romanticized the age of chivalry. The image shows the detail of a Gothic Revival brooch in the shape of a trefoil, a popular Gothic Revival style element, and tracery enameling.

## Sentimental Jewelry

Hair jewelry in the early Victorian era begins with hair under glass and in lockets, but by 1838 the hair-work jewelry craze had begun. Watch chains, bracelets, earrings, and brooches could all be made out of woven strands of a loved ones hair. The 1855 Paris exposition featured a full-length portrait of Queen Victoria made entirely out of human hair.

**Early Victorian Gothic Revival brooch** with taille d'epargne enameling, trefoil form.

**Portrait engraving** of Abraham Lincoln wearing a woven hair watch chain.

Even Abraham Lincoln wore a watch chain made out of human hair. It is prominently featured in an engraving done of him in 1861. The engraving shown in the image here is often called "the five dollar bill pose" because it is the likeness from which American five-dollar bills were made. Hair-work jewelry continues in popularity throughout the Victorian era.

## Rococo Revival

Empress Eugenie of France was largely responsible for the popularity of the Rococo Revival Style. The motifs of the Rococo Revival style are essentially the same as for the Rococo style. The main way to tell the difference between the two is that the Rococo Revival jewelry will be largely machine made, where Rococo jewelry will be almost entirely hand-made. It would seem that the Rococo style never really went completely out of style. Its cyma curves, bowknots, shells, and floral patterns continue in popularity well into the 20th century. The image shows a brooch with a gadrooned leaf and an acanthus leaf in a cyma curve typical of the Rococo Revival style.

**Early Victorian, Rococo Revival brooch**, rolled gold.

## Archeological Inspired Themes

Sometimes called late classicism, archeological inspired themes continue to be popular in jewelry long after other forms of decorative arts have moved on to new revivals. Continued interest in Pompeii and Herculaneum as travel itineraries helped to keep archeological themes popular. Jewelers in Naples seemed to be able to "unearth" ancient treasures on a continuing basis. They seemed quite willing to supply tourists with "ancient jewelry" with which to commemorate their travels; no one went home without a treasure. Cameos figure prominently in archeological themes, commonly showing various Roman or Greek deities carved from hard stone materials, shell, or lava. The image shows an early Victorian cameo of a bacchante with gutta percha accents.

In 1836 Fortunato Pio Castellani was invited to catalog Etruscan treasures recovered from Vulci, making exact replicas of Etruscan jewelry, which he sold out of his store in Rome. It is around this time that Etruscan themes are added to existing archeological jewelry. They created replicas of deities in techniques they copied from the Etruscan treasures. River Gods, sun Gods, griffons, blackamoors, birds, sirens, and other mythological creatures were among the many motifs they employed. The Castellani's were particularly interested in the gold working techniques of the Etruscans. When Castellani died in 1865, his sons Alessandro and Augusto, also jewelers, carried on the family tradition.

## Inspired by Science and Technology

Life changed dramatically in the 19th century as a result of the industrial revolution. Science gave man a new understanding of his world. Changing technology resulted in countless labor saving devices. It seems natural that people sought artistic expression of these new discoveries through the use of decorative arts. This use of science and technology as inspiration for novelty jewelry continues throughout the century.

Early Victorian, bacchante cameo, bronze figure with gutta percha accents.

Punch 1858

When Haley's Comet was successfully predicted to return in 1834, an industrializing world turned its attention to astronomy. King Frederick VI of Denmark even offered gold medals to anyone who discovered a new comet, and in 1847 Maria Mitchell of Nantucket, Massachusetts claimed the prize. The comet-watching couple pictured in an 1858 edition of *Punch* Magazine shown here is evidence of how long-lived comet watching became, making *comet jewelry* a near necessity for a lady's toilette.

Science and technology continue to influence novelty jewelry. The portrait miniatures of the late Georgian era begin to be replaced by the Daguerreotype, a photographic process introduced in 1840.

When a project began to lay a transatlantic telegraph cable in 1853, Charles Louis Tiffany sold watch fobs and paperweights made of cross-sections of the cable. It would seem that nothing escaped notice of jewelry designers looking for an opportunity to promote their trade using new motifs in jewelry.

1858 *Punch* comic of comet watchers. Caption reads "So fond of astronomy, that they are always on the balcony looking for the comet."

## Early Victorian Jewelry

While *tiaras* were still appropriate for the very wealthy and royalty, the average woman wore *ferronnières* and *aigrettes*. Ferronnieres were worn for both day and evening wear while aigrettes were worn in the evening. Hair ornaments were dressed up for eveningwear by weaving and tucking flowers, ribbons, and strands of beads into the hair.

Favorite earring styles include the pendeloque, but the longer, thinner pendant style is more common. Even though hairstyles fully covered the ears, numerous period Daguerreotypes and fashion plates show pendant earrings dangling below the gathers of hair that covered the ears. When earrings were made as part of a parurer, they usually mirrored the central motif on the necklace or bracelet, so some larger oval and round forms were made. The image shows five sisters with pendant style earrings dropping from beneath hair that completely covers their ears. The image dates between 1841 and 1855.

**Family portrait** of five sisters, c1840; two wearing pendant earrings.

**Engraving** of a brooch en *pampilles* from the Great Exhibition of 1851.

*Bodice ornaments*, mainly brooches, took many forms. The girandole style, which was a popular Georgian earring style, was now commonly worn for brooches, again featuring a central setting with three drops suspended below. Another popular style of brooch was set *en pampilles*. This style featured a brooch, usually of floral design with a series of cascading gemstones or pastes in graduated sizes attached below the brooch. For daytime, a woman might cross a piece of flat ribbon around her neck and secure it with her favorite brooch.

Cameos are still popular due to the influence of ongoing excavations, but novel materials are used. Lava cameos, carved mainly in the southern region of Italy near Pompeii, gain popularity. Coral cameos and brooches in deep shades of orange and red are also frequent, likely made a popular gem material by Froment-Meurice, a jeweler to Empress Eugenie.

*Rivière* style necklaces, chokers, and double-stranded necklaces continue in popularity. The central pendant is much larger than the rest of the beads, with the girandole style a favorite. If not part of a five-piece parurer, necklaces had at the very least matching earrings and bracelets. Slide-chain necklaces are quite long now, measuring up to 60 inches. Women wound their slide-chains around buttons, tucked them into dress pockets, and wore the slide at different lengths for fashion variety. The daguerrotypes show women with different ways of wearing their slide chains.

Early Victorian **woman** wearing a slide chain with pocket watch.

**Early Victorian man and woman** both wearing watch chains. Woman's watch chain has a slide that is fastened below the collar.

The Chatelaine is still a necessary piece of jewelry for women, although multiple chains suspended from the hook plate start to gain in popularity towards the end of the period, generally replacing the wide, hinged plates, popular in the late Georgian era. The image here is an engraving of a chatelaine exhibited at the Great Exhibition of 1851. Other chatelaines are featured in chapter 11.

Cuff bracelets continue in popularity. They are still tight fitting made mainly of metal with a central oval cluster or gem. Since bracelets were often made in matching parurers, there are many fine examples made almost entirely of materials like seed pearls, coral, turquoise, and lava.

Since stylish bodices now feature a deep "v-shape" at the waist, belt buckles are rarely worn. Shoe buckles are not popular either, likely because they would look too weighty without a belt buckle for balance, although some provincial examples from Germany continued to be worn as part jewelry suites.

**Engraving** of an early style chatelaine shown at the Great Exhibition of 1851.

# Popular Gems and Gem Materials

Diamonds never loose their popularity, although they are still considered appropriate for eveningwear, sometimes still foil-backed to enhance their brilliance. Topaz, amethyst, emeralds, turquoise, and seed pearls also continue to fashionable jewelry choices to accent the evening toilette.

Coral is added to the list of fashionable gem materials. Primarily harvested and carved in Southern Italy, coral was associated with the neo-classical styles copied from ancient jewelry and was then a likely substance for use in jewelry of the time. Also, numerous period travel magazines make references to tourists returning home with carved coral horns, which, when pointed towards an evil spirit, makes them run away.

Other novelty materials that became popular were vulcanized rubber, gutta percha, and bog oak. Charles Goodyear developed a process to stabilize rubber in 1849. Aside from its industrial uses, it was also used in jewelry and buttons by pressing it into molds, much like clay. Black in color, it does tend to yellow at the edges over the years. Vulcanized rubber continued to be popular well into the 1880s. Bloomingdale's still advertised vulcanized rubber jewelry in their 1886 catalog.

Gutta percha was another rubbery substance harvested from the various Malaysian trees. Gutta percha was originally imported from Calcutta in 1840. It is not as elastic as rubber and tends to become brittle with age. Nearly white when harvested, it was processed to an almost black color often for mourning jewelry. It was also formed by pressing the softened material into molds. The detail image of a bacchante cameo shown previously is a bronze molded portrait accented with generous amounts of gutta percha, perhaps giving it the look of a very ancient piece or simply trying to add a new popular substance to what was then a fairly common motif.

**Detail** of a brooch with gutta percha accents.

Bog oak resulted from long periods of immersion in the Irish peat bogs. When it dried it was a very hard, dark material, suitable for carving. It is sometimes difficult to tell the difference between bog oak and other hard, blackish materials used in jewelry, but bog oak generally has Irish motifs like clovers or harps. Originally hand-carved, technology allowed machine stamping of designs in bog oak by 1852.

Another novelty material was a porous substance mistakenly called lava. A hardened by-product of volcanic eruptions mixed with limestone, they are soft and easy to carve, making detailed, high relief sculptures. Using this lava by-product, ancient artisans carved all sorts of decorative elements, including cameos. Sometime during the early 19th century, these lava cameos became a popular substance for jewelry. An example of a lava cameo of the goddess Diana is shown.

**Early Victorian lava cameo** of the Roman Goddess Diana. (Author's collection)

Ivory has a new status. In the late Georgian era, ivory was basically used as a canvas for portraitures, and to make small necessaries for the etui. Ivory is now carved in the shape of hands, flowers, and cherubs then mounted in brooches, pendants, and earrings. Ivory was also used as the base material for piqué.

Micromosaics and pietra dura continue to be used for jewelry, although romantic themes abound. Religious themes such as the "anchor of hope", "the hand of God", and crosses were still produced.

Towards the end of the early Victorian era, around 1860, tortoise-shell jewelry becomes popular again, especially piqué. On occasion, amber was used as the base material for piqué jewelry.

While the use of amber in jewelry dates to antiquity, *faceted* amber beads are believed to originate in Northern Germany in the 18th century. Since amber was believed to cure diseases, faceted amber beads were frequently given as gifts. In keeping with his German custom, Prince Albert gave Queen Victoria faceted amber beads, making them a popular gift.

# Decorating, Finishing and Other Techniques

Gold and silver were scarce materials in the early 19th century. A new process, *electroplating*, allowed a thin layer of gold or silver to be deposited over a layer of base metal. In the United Startes, silver plating was introduced in 1840 with gold plating to follow in 1844. Electroplated gold and silver used much thinner layers of precious metal than the rolled gold and Sheffield plate introduced in the late Georgian era.

Another popular method of making a little bit of metal go a long way was filigree. Long used in provincial jewelry in Germany, France, Norway, Turkey, and India, it is difficult to pinpoint its rise in popularity in the early Victorian era. One possibility may be that since machine-made draw-wire is now common, it may have been a logical step from the coarse, hand-made, jasseron and cannetille of the earlier period.

The 1849 gold discovery in California, and in Australia in 1851 expanded supplies of gold, making its use for jewelry more common.

By 1835, much of the jewelry was made by machine die-stamped forms, die-stamped designs, or both, and ready to supply consumer demands. There is also an important change in the way gemstones are set. In the late Georgian era, gems were set in a spreading collet. This will begin to be replaced by the claw setting and by 1850 will be the most common form seen for setting gemstones. This is especially important for dating rings, which typically do not give collectors very many dating clues.

While all previous forms of enameling are still employed, taille d'epargne enameling is especially popular because of the way it resembles the tracery used in Gothic architecture. An example of this delicate enameling style is shown on page 22.

# Chapter 3
# Mid-Victorian Jewelry
## 1861 to 1880

## Historical Background

Some refer to the mid Victorian era as "The Grand Period." Over the twenty-year span, there were a dozen international exhibitions with an equal number of regional expositions and fairs, all touting the newest, best, and fastest technology. The early failure of the transatlantic cable was resolved and the telegraph was the worlds' first intercontinental means of communication. The Nevada Comstock lode would produce over $400 million dollars in gold and silver ore between 1859 and 1878. Archeological exactions at Priam, in Greece, yielded 9,000 pieces of gold jewelry, and precious metal artifacts in 1868.

Newspapers and magazines published the activities of the aristocracy and privileged as they travel to exotic destinations. Queen Victoria is named Empress of India in 1876. A new fascination with the Middle East sets in with a series of events starting in 1862, when 50 pieces of jewelry from the tomb of Queen Aah Hotep were on display at the Paris International Exhibition. Empress Eugenie of France attends the grand opening of the Suez Canal in 1869. Giuseppe Verdi writes Aida for the opening of the opera house in Cairo in 1871.

In 1861, *Frank Leslies Illustrated News* headlines with President Lincoln's inaugural ball. The front page was entirely devoted to who wore what with the first lady taking center stage. Wedding bells ring for Prince Edward of England and his consort Alexandra. At the end of the era, Thomas Edison would introduce the electric light bulb, which would change the way women adorned themselves for evening entertainment.

But the decade that began with hope, prosperity and grandeur was also filled with tragedy. Four years earlier, the Crimean War ended with a half a million European casualties. Then suddenly in 1861 Prince Albert died. Queen Victoria went into a life-long morning over the loss of her "beloved Albert". In the United States, the Civil War would claim 618,000 lives, and in 1865 President Lincoln was assassinated. Then in 1870, after loosing the Franco-Prussian war, the French government under Napoleon III collapsed. Both he and Empress Eugenie were exiled.

# Mid-Victorian Fashion Influences

In practice the average women dressed far more conservatively than the elite and wealthy. From about 1860 to 1869 ladies daytime wear included, collared necklines, sometimes tied with a bow. By 1870, the neckline dips enough to accommodate a locket or cross, suspended from a ribbon tied around the neck. The Basque bodice, which looks somewhat like an overcoat, usually buttoned or overlapped in the front and is frequently seen with a belt. The v-shaped waistline is less popular, which also allowed for the wearing of belts, again. Dropped shoulders are still popular. Bell shaped sleeves with billowing under sleeves are also common. It was considered inappropriate to wear low cut bodices or short sleeves for anything other than evening wear. In either event it did not prevent women from wearing bracelets to complete the toilette.

1865 *Peterson's Magazine* of a woman wearing a fashionable "Empire head-dress".

For eveningwear, the bodice is now draped with lace and accented with ribbons and flowers. The v-shaped waistline complimented the v-shaped bodice. The sweetheart neckline is also popular; both with short, puffy sleeves to finish the look. In most instances, the size of the social gathering dictated the length of the sleeve, with ¾ sleeves reserved for intimate dinner parties. Skirts begin to have flounces adding yet more volume and yet more weight. Ladies' skirts reach their fullest point around 1864. While many women continue to wear crinoline petticoats, the hoop skirt becomes popular, as the steel hoops are still much lighter than 40 layers of fabric. Aside from a short flirtation with bustles and trains, skirts trim down by 1881.

BALL HEAD-DRESS.

**Daytime fashions for 1865** with a sweetheart neckline (left) and a Basque bodice (right).

**Evening Fashions for 1865** from *Peterson's Magazine*.

For daytime, the ears remain partially covered until the 1870s when hair was swept back and up, but women continued to wear bonnets during the day. Early in the period, hairstyles for the evening show the ears. Evening hair fashions included clusters of flowers worn in the hair resembling hats. Strands of beads cover large buns worn at the nap of the neck, and ribbons woven and worn like small caps were dubbed the "Empire head-dress".

They would also attach cameos to the ribbons and wear them like a tiara. By 1870, women began to wear their hair in upsweeps with combs pushing their hair back behind the ears.

Up until 1864, as the proportions of ladies' clothing grow, the size of the jewelry also grows with brooches becoming larger, necklaces becoming bulkier, bracelets becoming wider, and earrings, when worn, are longer. As skirts became first more bell-shaped, and then more form fitting, the proportions of the jewelry also changed, becoming smaller.

1865 *Peterson's Magazine* of a woman wearing a cameo head-dress.

1870s Currier and Ives tinted engraving of a woman wearing a ribbon necklace with attached brooches, matching earrings.

# Popular Jewelry Styles and Forms

### Gothic, and Rococo Revival

Both Gothic Revival and Rococo Revival jewelry continued in popularity in the mid-Victorian era, although the popularity of Gothic Revival ended by 1870. The motifs did not change, so Gothic quatrefoils, drapery, and heraldic shields are still used as decorative elements in jewelry and the ever popular cyma curve with it's endless variations continued to be produced.

### Renaissance Revival Jewelry

The Victoria and Albert Museum was established with profits from the Great Exhibition of 1851. Originally called *The Museum of Manufactures*, it contained exhibits from the Great Exhibition. A decision was made to instead feature decorative arts from antiquity to the modern era and in 1857, the name was changed to *The Museum of Ornamental Art*. In particular the museum began adding historical pieces of decorative art.

What is important about this change is that for the first time, the average individual (or aspiring jewelry designer) could see the royal family's fabulous collection of renaissance jewelry, and drawings of jewelry by famous medieval designers. Renaissance Revival jewelry took its inspiration from these museum displays, resulting in motifs that included acorns, figural pendants, and numerous variations of shield-shaped brooches, pendants, and bracelet clasps. One image features a mid-Victorian mourning brooch in a shield shape accented with acorns.

Renaissance Revival jewelry dominated the Paris Exhibition of 1867 and featured quatrefoils and shield shapes, usually with a central figure or portrait, competed with pearl drops almost without exception.

Mid-Victorian Renaissance Revival mourning brooch of dyed horn.

Engraving of a Renaissance Revival brooch by Rouvenat, shown at the Paris Exposition of 1867.

Engraving of a Renaissance Revival brooch by Massin, shown at the Paris Exposition of 1867.

### Archeological Themes

Greek, Roman, and Etruscan themes are a continuation of earlier styles, their popularity kept alive in part due to the on going excavations and new discoveries in Priam in 1868. The Castellanis exhibited their Etruscan Revival jewels at both the Paris Exposition in 1867 and in the 1876 Centennial Exhibition in Philadelphia.

In his 1868 book, *Notes and Sketches of the Paris Exhibition*, George Augustus Sala writes:

". . .I perforce omitted to mention many exhibitors whom it would be most unjust to pass over in silence. At least half-a-dozen times I have mentioned the name of M. Castellani, of Rome, as one of the foremost manufacturers of antique jewellery in Europe, or perhaps the world; but I have not yet told you what M. Castellani has to show. May the following brief paragraph make some amends. The Castellani exhibit is of a duplex nature. The first category is formed of that wonderfully beautiful "Etruscan" jewellery, from antique models, in the production of which he has long held the first rank among Continental goldsmiths. The second moiety of M. Castellani's display is devoted to a very curious and suggestive collection of the gold and silver ornaments worn by the Italian peasantry and lower middle classes."

Mid-Victorian Etruscan granulation brooch.

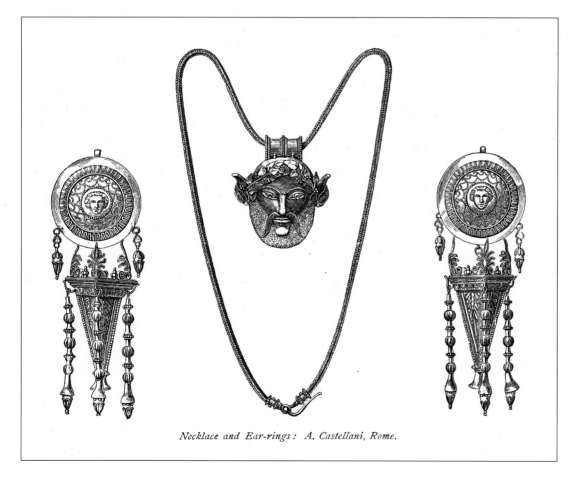

*Necklace and Ear-rings : A. Castellani, Rome.*

**Engraving** of Etruscan Revival jewelry by Castellani, shown at the Centennial Exhibition of 1876.

## Exotic Themes

Western Europeans had a long history of fascination with decorative art from the near east, middle east, and far east.

The Algerian style was popular when France declared Algeria a local administrative unit of France. This increased French colonization gave jewelers new inspiration in the form of traditional Moorish arabesques, fishes, stars, fringe, knots, chains, and tassels. Algerian themes find their way into jewelry from the late 1850s and continued in popularity until about 1870 when Empress Eugenie was exiled. One image features a mid-Victorian brooch with filigree, tassels, and chain.

Inspired by the display of Queen Aah-Hotep's jewels in 1862, jewelers like John Brodgen of London, created Egyptian Revival pieces for the Paris Exhibition of 1867. In the same year Isabel Glyn played Cleopatra at the Princess theatre, adding to the Egyptian Revival fever. The trend continues as Paris Jeweler, Emile Phillipe introduces his Egyptian designs at the Centennial Exposition in 1876. Another image is a Currier and Ives print showing a main-stream interest in exotic Egyptian jewelry. The crescent-shsaped brooch shown is a more modest version of the style.

Another exotic jewelry motif becomes popular when Queen Victoria became Empress of India in 1876. Tiger claws trimmed with gold are now a favorite adornment. They are worn in complete parurers and also made into useful items like vinaigrettes.

**Mid-Victorian Algerian style brooch**, filigree, tassels, and chain in silver.

**Egyptian Revival brooch** by Phillipe, exhibited at the Paris Exposition of 1867.

*Egyptian Brooches: Emile Philippe.*

**Egyptian Revival brooch** by Brogden, exhibited at the Paris Exposition of 1867.

**Egyptian Revival brooch**, rolled gold, Damascene finish.

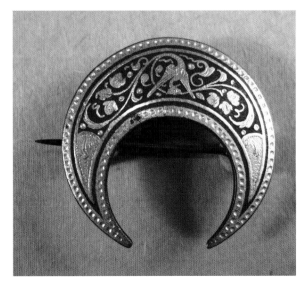

**Currier and Ives portrait** of an "Egyptian Beauty" wearing traditional jewelry.

### Inspired by Science and Technology

*On the Origin of Species*, published by Charles Darwin in 1859 was not simply the focal point of scientific debate in the 19th century. His observations of mutations in nature pointed the decorative arts community in the direction of naturalistic motifs. Insects, birds, and butterflies were popular motifs for jewelry. *The Jeweler's Circular and Horological Review* of 1879 had this to say about insect jewelry:

"A fly is the fancy ornament of the day, a pretty little fly, so skillfully and perfectly imitated that it looks like life."

In the same issue we also find that:

"The newest design in conch shell earrings is a shell from which bends a tiny Nereid (sea nymph) trailing her fingers over the brim, as if trying to wet them in the sea"

A London magazine published a satirical engraving in response to *designs after nature*.

1873 *Punch* Magazine satire on naturalistic fashions for women.

MR. PUNCH'S DESIGNS AFTER NATURE.
GREAT SENSATION FOR THE AQUARIUM—*COIFFURE OCTOPUS*.

### Mourning Jewelry

Victorian society had strict codes of dress for the period of mourning. The tragedies of the era paved the way for a renewed interest in mourning jewelry. When a loved one or relative passed away, adult women were expected to wear mourning attire, which meant that in the United States, women dressed entirely in black. Customs varied somewhat in England and Continental Europe, but it was generally recognized that the mourning period should vary depending on the relationship to the deceased. There were also stages of mourning; usually divided into three periods. During the initial period of mourning, jewelry was not worn at all. It is suggested that any pins and buckles were to be made of jet. Later, entirely black jewelry could be worn and during the final stage of mourning, black jewelry could feature pearl and amethyst. Even while mourning, women still sought to be stylish. The image shown on page 30 is an example of Renaissance Revival jewelry, which conveniently doubled as a mourning brooch.

### Sentimental Jewelry

The hair work jewelry craze that began in the late 1830s continues in popularity in the mid-Victorian era. Brooches, bracelets, watch chains, and fobs continue to be woven entirely of human hair. It is a common misconception that hair jewelry is mourning jewelry. Codes of dress dictated that mourning jewelry had to be black. While a black locket with an interior compartment for hair could be considered mourning jewelry, a brooch, ring, or pendant with a visible locket of hair would not.

### Novelty and Sporting Jewelry

While social etiquette in the beginning of the Grand Period frowned upon wearing too much jewelry during the day, by 1879, novelty and sporting motifs in jewelry are numerous and this etiquette is generally ignored. Horseshoes, owls, buckets, drums, barrels, animal heads, hearts, and hands, are just a few of the motifs and styles found in period catalogs by 1880. The image shown is an example of a horseshoe brooch, a popular motif for jewelry.

Mid-Victorian sporting motif jewelry, horseshoe-shape, 2.75 in. long.

## Mid-Victorian Jewelry

The most noticeable addition to earrings is the introduction of the post back (U.S. patent #122,328). This allowed small knots, balls, and squares to be worn directly against the ear lobe. Hoop earrings make an appearance in Peterson's magazine in 1870. By 1878 hoop earring have acquired drops and fringe.

Demi-parurers were marketed in the form of brooch and earring sets.

Several innovations were introduced for necklaces. A patent was filed to connect seed pearl necklaces with metal rings instead of the tradition method that used horsehair (U.S. patent #23,760). It made the necklace more durable and makes it easier to date later examples. We also see more fringe necklaces, inspired from Etruscan revival styles. The book chain necklace featured wide, flattened, rolled gold links that resembled Renaissance regalia.

Lower necklines gave women more freedom to wear lockets. Most could hold a daguerreotype, a locket of hair, or both. Micromosaic brooches were now fashionably formed in diamond shapes and squares.

Bracelets could be made in mesh wire or bangles. Bracelets with overlapping ends called bypass bracelets are advertised by 1879.

1870s Currier and Ives portrait of a woman wearing a ribbon necklace and locket.

# Popular Gems and Gem Materials

Jet, bog oak, vulcanite, dyed horn, and gutta percha continue to be popular mainly because of the amount of time women spent wearing mourning attire.

Amber, ivory, coral, and carnelian become more popular as they were common materials found in ancient jewelry and were thus used by jewelers creating archeological inspired pieces.

Turquoise was featured by prominent French jewelers at the 1867 Paris Exhibition and was considered to be a Turkish influence. Garnets become very popular with entire parurers of jewelry set with dozens and dozens of these tiny red jewels.

Naturalistic motifs in jewelry inspired the use of seashells, sea beans, real insects, bird feathers, and even hummingbird heads.

A new material, celluloid, is introduced to the jewelry industry in 1876. It seemed to have a thousand uses as it could be molded and colored to look like tortoise, coral, horn, jet, or ivory. It became a low-priced alternative for budget conscious women. The image features celluloid combs in an 1878 jeweler's wholesale catalog.

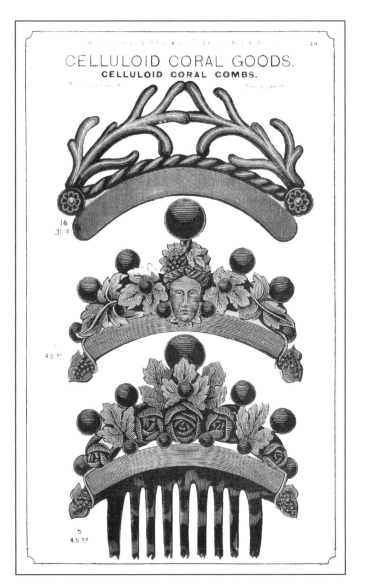

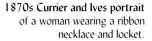

CELLULOID CORAL GOODS.
CELLULOID CORAL COMBS.

1878 wholesale catalog advertising "celluloid coral goods".

# Decorating, Finishing, and Other Techniques

Since the Gothic Revival style continues in popularity, taille d'epargne enameling was used in jewelry until about 1870.

The Castallanis experimented with granulation, filigree, and bloomed gold, in an attempt to recreate these ancient jewelry techniques in their jewelry. Since they were scholars and lectured frequently on Etruscan decorative arts, there were many imitators of their techniques.

A new type of setting, called a gypsy setting featured a gemstone that was sunk into the surface of the piece. It is introduced around 1878 and was employed as decoration for rings, lockets, pendants and brooches. In 1879 Ripley, Howland, and Company advertise their patented platinum-tipped diamond settings. This made diamonds look whiter in their settings.

A new form of brooch is introduced. Modern collectors call them bar pins, but period catalogs from the late 1870s called them shawl pins. They are longer and more rectangular than normal brooches. At the same time, Limoges porcelain brooches give a new look to cameos. They are hand painted with neo-classical style elements and continued in popularity into the late Victorian era.

1879 advertising of platinum-tipped settings.

# Chapter 4
# Late Victorian Jewelry
## 1881 to 1901

## Historical Background

Though the Congress of Vienna established boundaries for much of Europe after Napoleon Bonaparte's defeat, those boundaries and their forms of government continued to change throughout much of the 19th century. Many of Europe's aristocrats were forced to sell their possessions often to have money to flee their crumbling monarchies. Some refer to this time as The Aesthetic Period.

France, had long been considered a major influence on fashion, but when the French government of Napoleon III collapsed in 1870, he and his fashionable wife, Eugenie were exiled.

But where there is tragedy, there is often opportunity. Between 1848 and 1887, Charles Louis Tiffany made five major purchases of jewelry from Europe's titled elite. Most publicized was his purchase of one-third of the French Crown Jewels, purchased from the exiled Empress Eugenie in 1887.

It appeared that the only remaining monarch stable enough to influence fashion was Queen Victoria. But by 1880, Queen Victoria was still in mourning for her "beloved Albert", and had little desire to influence fashion. Her daughter-in-law, Alexandra had few opportunities to influence fashion when Queen Victoria ordered mourning dress at court in 1880, nearly 20 years after Albert's death. Queen Victoria never emotionally recovered from the death of her husband. She continued to mourn her loss until her own death in 1901.

It is not difficult to see that those seeking a source for fashion influences began to turn their attentions to nouveau riche like opera singers, theatrical performers, artists, and wives of wealthy American industrialists.

Other fashion influences would come from an unlikely source, one of the last remaining exotic destinations, the western United States. In 1886, the South Kensington Museum in England displayed an exhibit of Native American Jewelry. William Cody's Wild West Show peaked the interest of Europeans, featuring three tours to England and the Continent. The Wild West Show was part of the tribute to Queen Victoria's Golden Jubilee in 1887. In total she saw the show three times.

Tourists interested in traveling to the wild west found that Fred Harvey had already established his chain of motels and restaurants along the route of the Atchison, Topeka and Santa Fe Railroad. By 1887, there were 17 Harvey Houses in the southwest. Aside from food and lodging, tourist could purchase souvenirs, including jewelry, from the Native Americans who created turquoise and silver jewelry to sell to the tourists.

World's fairs and regional exhibitions continued to be a major source of discovery for a growing middle class. The 1893 Columbian Exhibition was the first electrically lit world's fair. Thomas Edison's light bulb was only two years old when the Savoy Theatre in London became the first electrically lit theatre in 1881. For the fashion conscious, this meant that colors that looked pleasing under candlelight looked garish under incandescent light.

# Fashion Influences

The high standing collar is the most common collar worn in the late Victorian era, rising to just below the chin by 1897. Tying a scarf around the neck or attaching a bow to the collar achieved some variation. This somewhat limits jewelry choices for women, making bar brooches the common choice for daytime wear. If lockets were worn, they were usually worn with a neck chain that sat just above the bosom. The high standing collar limited earring choices, too, so small drops or studs completed the daytime outfit.

Bodices in the late Victorian era are very tight and form fitting until about 1893. From about 1877 to 1883, the Polonaise bodice is popular for both day and eveningwear. Still form fitting, it drops to mid-thighs, so belts are not worn until the Basque bodice is popular again from 1883 to 1888. The Basque bodice, ending just below the waistline is often seen with a belt. By 1893, form-fitting bodices end at the waist. Belts and vinaigrettes are a popular fashion accent for the rest of the era. For that perfect hourglass shape, ladies could purchase pads to make their hips look wider. In the last decade of the 19th century, a looser French style, blouse front becomes popular, giving women at least the look of less confined clothing. Ladies do wear lower cut bodices for eveningwear, revealing at most, the upper chest area. This is the only opportunity to wear necklaces.

The drop sleeve is gone by 1883. Sleeves are very straight, getting tighter until about 1889. At this point, the top of the sleeve is slightly puffy reaching its fullest point in 1893. By 1900 the puff portion of the sleeve is much smaller. All variations easily accommodate bracelets, but by 1889 bracelets are much thinner than those from the mid-Victorian era.

Skirts for most of the era drop straight with some fullness and limited trimming at the feet. The bustle is still popular until 1893, but long trains are mercifully only appropriate for the evening toilette. When puffy sleeves reach their fullest point in 1893, the skirts are flared to give the look more balance.

Women now wear hats, not bonnets. For most of the period, hair is pulled back, usually in a bun. Combs and hatpins are important elements for the last twenty years of the 19th century.

1887 **portrait** of Lily Langtry and Sarah Bernhardt wearing late Victorian fashions.

**Portrait** of young woman in fashionable clothing around 1897, wearing a sautoir.

**Portrait** of a young woman in fashionable clothing around 1893, wearing a hair comb and brooch.

# Popular Jewelry Styles and Forms

### Exotic Themes

The fascination with Egyptian, Algerian, and Turkish themes continue to inspire jewelry fashions. Jewelry of the era features portraits of Egyptian rulers; bypass bracelets wind around the wrist and terminate with snakeheads. Turkish daggers and Algerian knots are common. Acorns are another decorative element found dangling from earrings and bracelets.

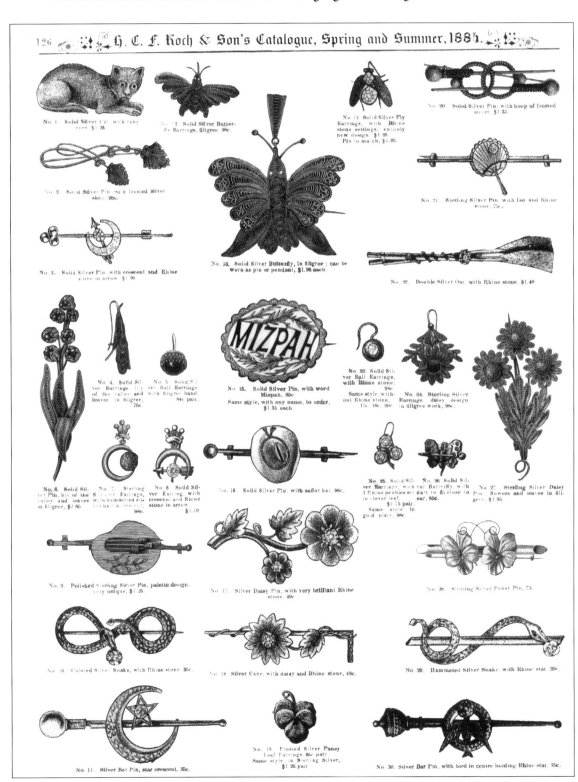

1885 Koch and Sons catalog showing popular motifs for jewelry.

The opening of *The Mikado* at the Savoy in 1885, inspires it's own themes as period catalogues offer *Mikado* brooches featuring fans, bamboo, and faces of delicate looking geishas.

Jewelry made by Native Americans will serve as inspiration for the developing Arts & Crafts movement of the late 19th century. A ¾ length photograph of Lavinia (Vinnie) Ellen Ream shows her wearing a Navajo squash blossom necklace with matching earrings, an indication of the rising popularity of this type of jewelry in the mid-Victorian era. (Ms. Ream sculpted the statue of Abraham Lincoln in the U.S. Capitol rotunda)

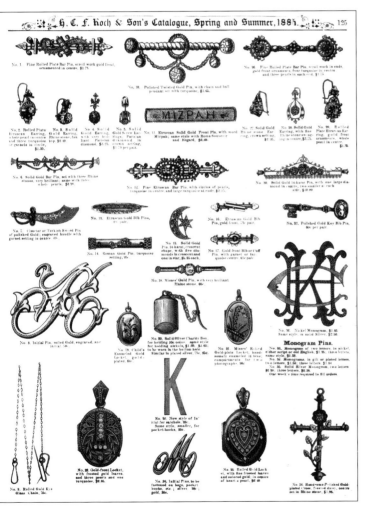

**Late Victorian silver plated brooch** advertised as a "Mikado Brooch".

**Late 1870s portrait** of Vinnie Sulptress Ream wearing Navajo Squash Blossom necklace, matching earrings.

1885 Koch and Sons catalog showing popular motifs for jewelry.

### Renaissance Revival Themes

The popularity of shield-shaped forms continues until about 1890. The shapes and engraved surfaces could be combined in endless varieties for the female consumer.

### Archeological Themes

Some designers, like Peter Carl Fabergé, favored the neo-classical style, producing exquisite examples for the Russian Imperial Court. Fabergé favored guilloché and basse-taille enameling. Much less elaborate copies were marketed by jewelers through catalogs and stores. Other archeological motifs included roman coils and urns, and horns that were believed to ward off evil.

Etruscan Revival styles are still popular until the late 1880s, with granulation and filigree being the most common examples of the style.

Sulfide cameos and reverse painted cameos add new popularity to existing cameo styles. Both are etched from the back and either filled with plaster as in the case of sulfides or painted.

Late Victorian reverse painted portrait with a neo-classical figure, chain safety.

### Colonial Revival

Inspired by the Centennial Exhibition in 1876, colonial revival themes could take any number of expressions. *Colonial* was loosely defined as referring to the styles popular during the colonization of the United States. It was anything from Gothic to Federal and typically combined styles the result of which was often neither. The trend is expressive of the late Victorian era, where lines between styles are no longer well defined.

Examples of this style of Jewelry could contain old or ancient pieces, like coins or watch movements from 18th century pocket watches. In other examples, porcelain cameos were painted with 18th century portraits.

### Sentimental

Very little hair jewelry is made and marketed in the late Victorian era. Other sentimental forms like the mizpah were very popular around 1880. Mizpah has its origins in the Old Testament. It was a watchword for the phrase "The Lord watch between me and thee when we are absent one from another".

Link bracelets were sold with heart-shaped padlocks and keys (dubbed "engagement bracelets"). A crescent moon and bee was a called a honeymoon brooch, although all types of crescent brooches were popular.

Late Victorian "engagement bracelet", rolled gold.

Late Victorian crescent moon and star motif, set with garnets, rolled gold. (Courtesy of Roberta Knauer Mullings, G.G.).

## Novelty

Here was another opportunity for variety as jewelers made brooches and stickpins with animals like frogs, lizards, turtles, birds, and birds in flight. Horseshoes and wishbones as good luck charm also gained in popularity in the late Victorian era. Pavé-set starbursts make their appearance in the late Victorian era. They continue in popularity into the 20th century.

**Late Victorian bird-in-flight motif** with wishbone, verso with "Mizpah", faux pearl, glass, rolled gold.

**Late Victorian sporting motif**, horseshoe, 0.75 in. long.

The era also saw a rise in social organizations. Every organization had its own symbols and jewelers were anxious to cater to the growing demand for emblematic pins, watch fobs, lockets, signet rings and charms. The Daughters of the American Revolution was one such organization. Founded on October 11, 1890, the image shows an early emblematic brooch/pendant dated 9-22-91, less than a year after the organization was formed.

For the more independent spirit, jewelers stocked supplies of starburst, Roman coils, monogram rings, brooches, and pins; no whimsy was left behind.

**Late Victorian Roman coil brooch**, faux turquoise, gold.

**Emblematic brooch** of the Daughters of the American Revolution, verso with manufacture and date of 1891. (Courtesy of Roberta Knauer Mullings, G.G.)

## Late Victorian Jewelry

While there are some very early examples of *hatpins*, they began to be produced in large numbers in the late 19th century when women no longer wore bonnets that were kept in place with ribbons that tied under the chin.

The *aigrette*, long out of fashion, is popular again for eveningwear.

Earrings with short drops or small studs work well with high standing collars. They begin to appear in catalogs by 1881, gaining in popular as the next two decades progressed.

Tight fitting chokers of multi-strand beads were worn mostly with evening dresses by 1881. By 1889, book chain necklaces are still featured in catalogues, but not as frequently as in the previous two decades. Long glass bead necklaces, similar to the late Georgian sautoir become popular in the 1890s. Women also worn princess length gold and silver bead necklaces, 17 – 20 inches long.

The rectangular shawl pins of the late 1870s have evolved into slightly shorter, bar pins. Bar pins remain the most common daytime jewelry item and jewelers offered countless variations. By 1889, jewelers also sold bar pins made exclusively for babies and small girls. Another popular feature was a brooch with an attached chain and stickpin for additional safety. They make an appearance in the early 1880s and continue to be made, although typically with more round or oval brooches. Small bar pins were sold in linked sets of three.

While some wide bracelets continue to be advertised, thinner bracelets compliment the trimmed down look of women's clothing styles. The most popular styles are those that overlap with decorative terminals, like beads, cubes, and rams' heads. Period catalogues also begin to feature bead bracelets.

In the last decade of the 19th century, the chatelaine is fashionable again. It is not the necessity of earlier times. The various attachments were still functional, but it was viewed more as a fashion accessory. It was also fashionable to wear vinaigrettes suspended from the belt on a chain.

**Portrait** of Helen Garrettson wearing a chatelaine, c. 1900.

# Popular Gems and Gem Materials

Diamonds never loose their popularity, but not everyone could afford diamonds. Brazilian pebble, actually clear quartz, was advertised as a convincing substitute for diamonds.

Jet, bog oak, onyx, and vulcanite (now simply called rubber) continue to be used for jewelry, but the forms are much more simple. Bead bracelets, drop earrings, and simple rectangular bar brooches are more common than ornately carved pieces. A new black material, crepe stone, is also added to the acceptable list of mourning jewelry. It was actually matte finished glass with a wavy surface.

Many natural substances enjoy popularity including seashells, sea bean, and branch coral.

Although the first synthetic ruby is developed in 1885, it does not become commonplace in jewelry until just before the turn of the century.

The other important innovation is the power-bruiting machine. Developed in 1891, it could produce a new cut of diamond, the Old European cut. This machine was powerful enough to allow the girdle of the diamond to be cut round, replacing the mine-cut diamond having a square face and rounded corners.

In general, the preference for evening wear is for light and colorless gemstones that seem to display more brilliance when worn in newly electrically lit opera houses and theatres.

# Decorating, Finishing and Other Techniques

Invisible settings also complimented the fashion preference for light and colorless gemstones. Lighter color preferences make silver and platinum more popular metals. There are also mixed metal techniques, inspired by the Japanese metal working arts that combine rose gold, white gold, and yellow gold in exotic motifs.

In 1886 Tiffany introduces a six-prong setting that raises the diamond above the setting allowing more light to reflect from the gem stone.

Gold and Silver filigree, continue to be popular as the technique works well with delicate design preferences. Wire wrapping was a jewelry fad that continued to be popular into the early 20th century. Branch coral, seashells, and sea beans dangled from fancifully wound gold and rolled gold wire.

Since the modern safety clasp had yet to be invented, many jewelers began attaching a small chain to brooches which would attach separately with a safety pin or stick pin, adding a safety feature to the jewelry.

# Chapter 5
# La Belle Époque
## 1880 to 1914

## Historical Background

The period between 1880 and 1914 was considered to be the golden age for Europe's aristocracy and elite. Most of the royals whose countries survived the turmoil of the previous decades lived plentiful lifestyles. In the United States, the industrial revolution created a wealthy class, free of encumbrances like personal income tax and property tax. In short, there was money to be spent on opulence. This era is usually referred to as the Belle Époque. The term is used here as a way to tie together several decorative arts movements that share little in common other than the time at which they occur.

The Belle Époque was interrupted when the assassination of Archduke Franz Ferdinand of Austria triggered World War One in 1914. By the time the war had ended in 1918, a staggering 20 million civilians and soldiers had died. The United States joined the war in 1917. Families hung small flags in the windows with a central blue star to show support for their loved ones serving overseas. In the aftermath of the war, many jewelers and silversmiths went out of business, unable to recover from the economic losses of the war.

Another kind of battle was won in 1920 when the United States Congress passed the nineteenth amendment giving women the right to vote. The colors of the movement, green, violet, and white can sometimes be found in period jewelry.

## Fashion Influences

High necklines for daytime wear continue in popularity from 1900 to about 1909. The neckline and bodice are accented with a fichu, a lace shawl or collar that drapes over the shoulders and fastened in the front with brooch. Women also wore necklaces with pendants over the high collars, with the pendant falling at the small of the neck. Around 1912, v-shaped, draped bodices allowed for the wearing of bead necklaces, ranging from chokers up to 17 inches long. From this point to the end of the period, women wore rounded necklines, v-shaped necklines, and open collared shirts for daytime wear. All could accommodate short necklaces.

Although bodices of the era look loose fitting, they are actually tightly corseted, with soft gathers of fabric falling over the bust line to the waist, and belted. Some variations featured a more tailored look with paneled bodices that fell straight to the ground with no break at the waistline. The style allowed for the continued popularity of the sautoir.

The flared skirts were increasingly drawn closer to the ankle, reaching their tightest around 1912. Sometimes called a "hobble shirt", some designers featured crossed panels that opened in the front allowing women to take a normal stride. The length of the skirt continues to rise reaching mid-calf by the end of World War I.

Paris fashions for 1912, ladies wearing hobble skirts.

**Woman** wearing a house dress and fichu, 1904.

**Lily Langtry** wearing a "V" neck collar, pearl sautoir and choker necklace.

## Edwardian Jewelry, 1901 to 1909

Edward becomes king of England and his lovely wife Alexandra is Queen. Victoria had long withdrawn from social circles so the Princess Alexandra had influence on fashion well before her coronation in 1902. Her preferences leaned more toward neo-classical revival styles of the late Victorian era featuring high necklines with bead chokers, white on white, delicate, invisible settings, garland style necklaces and long ropes of pearls. A brooch with a crown above double hearts was a popular symbol of their coronation. But fashion influence in the late 19th and early 20th centuries now comes from diverse sources. Two other art movements born in the late 19th century, Arts and Crafts and Art Nouveau flourish in the early 20th century.

# Arts and Crafts Jewelry, 1880 to 1920

The Arts and Crafts movement was founded in England by William Morris. It was in one aspect a response to the lack of individual creativity that was lost during the industrial revolution. William Morris was interested in the medieval system of guilds, where craftsmen spent years to perfect their trades. To emphasize craftsmanship, Arts and Crafts jewelers, usually worked in semi-precious and non-precious gems and metals. Designers used very simple, non-representational motifs that did not compete with the aesthetics of well-executed designs. The movement spread throughout the artistic communities of Europe and the United States. The *Jeweler's Circular and Horological Review* mentions a popular bracelet style where the hammering marks are left visible to show hand workmanship in their 1879 edition.

There was a problem with items made entirely by hand; they were costly to make and expensive to buy. When coupled with the use of semi-precious and non-precious materials, it required that the buyer have rather a sophisticated knowledge of jewelry. For nouveau riche Americans it simply did not the fit their image of an abundant lifestyle. For the middle class, the items were too expensive. In order to market these items to the middle class, companies like Liberty and Company created mass-produced versions of their hand-made pieces.

**Arts and Crafts brooch** with machine-made, hand-hammered look, brass and glass.

**Navajo woman** wearing squash blossom necklace and concha belt in photograph by Edward Curtis, 1904.

Another influence on the Arts and Crafts movement was jewelry produced for tourists by Native Americans. The design qualities of irregularly shaped gemstones along with the lack of precision complimented the ideals of the Arts and Crafts movement. Many were inspired by the handcrafted look and simple design qualities of Native American jewelry.

# Art Nouveau Jewelry, 1885 to 1915

The Art Nouveau movement on the other hand sought to capture the vitality of nature, not copy its forms. Art Nouveau artisans did not seek to represent a flower, but rather to show the life force that urged it to grow. René Lalique embraced this first truly new art movement. It was a short-lived movement, flourishing from about 1885 to about 1915. Its influence can be attributed, in part, to Japanese fine and decorative art. Lalique was also influenced by the Symbolist writers of the time. He sought to depict the "veiled essence" of his subject matter, the idea behind the form. One of the most important subjects was woman in her many guises such as nurturer, seductress, innocent. Art Nouveau jewelry attracts international attention when Lalique sponsors his own exhibit at the 1900 Paris Exposition. He sold the entire collection to Calouste Gulbenkian, a wealthy Armenian businessman. Today the collection resides at the Gulbenkian Museum in Portugal. Lalique also acquired Sarah Bernhardt as a patron. Ms. Bernhardt was a popular American actress who influenced fashions in the late 19th century.

Art Nouveau had many critics in Great Brittain and the United States. The 1910 Encyclopedia Britannica had this to say about Art Nouveau:

> "In Paris, the taste for the contortions of what is called *art nouveau* has led to the errection, here and there, of ugly and eccentric fronts with preposterous ornamental details; but the invasion of this element is only partial and will probably not prove other than a passing phase."

It is apparent that whiplash curves, women with wildly flowing tresses, metamorphasizing butterflies, rattlesnakes, bats, and exotic flowers, did not have universal appeal.

There is often confusion between Arts and Crafts and Art Nouveau jewelry. René Lalique's style was flamboyant and fluid. Lluis Masriera, a jeweler from Barcelona, Spain, created a slightly different interpretation. His art nouveau pieces, many executed in pliqué-à-jour enamel resemble tiny stained glass windows. In general, Spanish art nouveau has a strong neo-Gothic element. Gothic tracery and quatrefoils take on fluid, dimensional expression. Angels and gargoyles are spirited and lively, giving Art Nouveau vitality to an ancient style.

The English approach to Art Nouveau was much more reserved. There is often little visible difference between English Art Nouveau pieces and Arts and Crafts pieces. Austrian interpretation of Art Nouveau showed fluid movement and vitality, but used more non-representational or more stylized use of form. The net effect was almost a hybrid of both Arts and Crafts and Art Nouveau. Many designers, like Louis Comfort Tiffany worked in both the Arts and Crafts and Art Nouveau styles.

Art Nouveau watch pin in sterling silver, front and back views.

Both forms used enameling techniques. Both forms used freshwater pearl drops. Also, Arts and Crafts tended to use more cabochon cut gemstones. Knowing the country of origin, the designer, and time period of production can make the identification definitive but it is easy to see that when taken as a whole, deciding whether an unsigned piece is one or the other is simply a matter of opinion.

**Sterling silver bar pin** by Unger Brothers, verso maker's mark; Art Nouveau or Arts and Crafts?

## Novelty Jewelry

When Alice Nielsen starred in the comic opera, *The Fortune Teller*, she wore a snake bracelet that was later made popular by enterprising jewelers like A.C. Becken. The "Alice Nielsen Bracelet" appears in Becken's 1902 jewelry catalog and is likely responsible for the return of the snake motif in bracelets and rings.

Although Alexander Dumas was a popular *early* 19th century French writer, translations of his novels were not readily available until the late 19th century. His novel *Louise de La Vallière* was about a mistress to Louis XIV of France. It talks about the necklace and jeweled pendant designed for her, now named the lavallière. La Vallière necklaces make an appearance around 1905 and La Vallière pendants around 1914. The 1913 Baird-North catalog features the lavallière necklace with uneven drops, called the négligée style.

Jewelry inspiration came from everywhere and anywhere. The 1903 popular song *Shine on Harvest Moon* was quickly translated into a jewelry motif when Macy's advertised the harvest moon brooch in their 1904 catalogs. This differs from the crescent moon seen earlier, as the harvest moon brooch is long and narrow. Macy's sold it with a single row of diamonds in platinum-topped gold.

1902 A. C. Becken catalog advertising the Carmen adjustable bracelet and the Alice Nielsen snake bracelet.

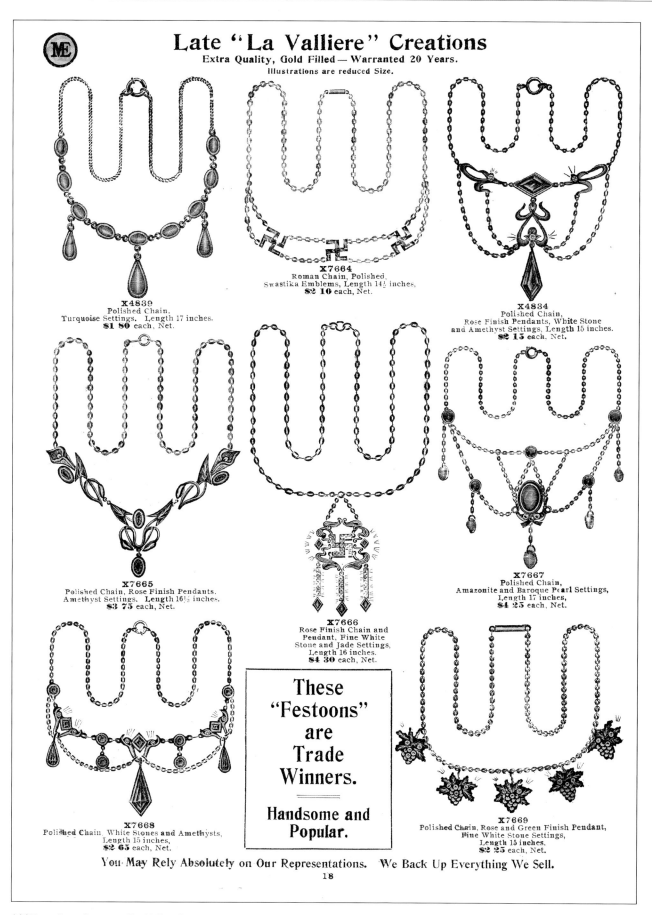

1907 catalog advertising "La Valliere" necklaces and festoon necklaces with various pendants and period good luck charms.

Another song, *There's a Little Blue Star in the Window*, written in 1918 highlighted the practice of hanging a banner in the window for a member of the armed forces serving overseas. Merchants introduced brooches, pendants, and bracelets featuring a small blue star bordered in red.

Good-luck symbols like clovers, horseshoes, wishbones, and the Greek swastika, a symbol of prosperity, were also popular themes for pendants, brooches, rings, and watch fobs and charms.

The popular Kewpie doll introduced in 1909 shows up in Sterling Kewpie brooches by 1913.

World War One "In Service" pin, fabric insignia, 14 karat, 0.50 in. diameter.

1918 Sheet music cover for *There's a Little Blue Star in the Window.*

# Belle Époque Jewelry, 1880 to 1914

Hatpins, now a fashion staple begin to appear in catalogs around 1900. Their themes mirrored other themes in jewelry. They were also sold in sets that included matching necklaces and bracelets.

For daytime wear, earrings could be small hoops, or endless varieties of balls, knots, pendant drops, or single brilliants. There were also *lavallière* style earrings. Non-pierced varieties with screw backs were widely advertised.

A new type of expandable bracelet, called the Carmen bracelet, made an appearance in 1902. It expanded to accommodate the hand and then contracted once fitted on the wrist. Chain bracelets with padlocks, often heart-shaped continue in popularity until about 1905. Almost Art Deco in appearance, delicate link bracelets, either saw-pierced or having the look of saw piercing start to appear around 1917.

There are several innovations in necklaces. The La Vallière style likely inspired the renewed popularity of the garland style necklace, called the festoon necklace at the time. Ribbon necklaces were also advertised for daytime wear in the second decade of the 20th century. Some styles features spring rings so ladies could change the pendant. The tango necklace, made popular by the risqué dance of the same name was advertised as a glass bead necklace that dropped to just above the waistline. Short necklaces in graduated beads of gold, silver, and pearl were popular accents to the new open "vee" and rounded, daytime necklines.

Styles for brooches were diverse and numerous. Any style or motif that appeared in other jewelry forms appeared in brooches. Since it is now acceptable for a lady to wear v-neck collars during the day, Baird-North advertises "vee" pins that attach to the newly popular neckline in their 1913 catalog.

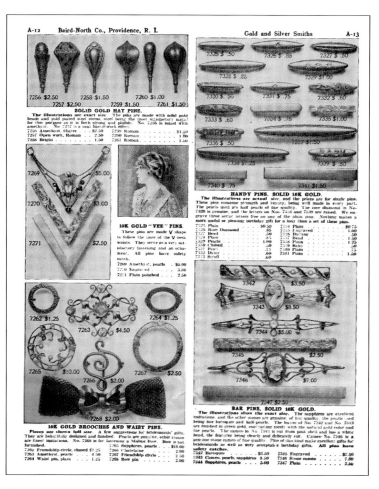

1913 Baird-North catalog showing hat pins, "V" Brooches, and bar pins.

# Popular Gems and Gem Materials

By 1905 cultured pearls are introduced commercially. Natural pearls were affordable only to the very wealthy, but cultured pearls are within the means of the middleclass. The preference for light and colorless gemstones continue with diamonds topping the list. Aquamarine, peridot, amethyst, moonstone, sapphire, and opal were all popular for eveningwear. If worn during the day, they were limited in quantity to perhaps three or four gems at the most.

For the budget conscious, onyx, cat's eye, Bakelite, sea shells, sea bean, branch coral, mother-of-pearl, gold stone glass, and turquoise could be worn during the day.

# Decorating, Finishing and Other Techniques

All types of translucent enamels are popular as a result of both the Art Nouveau and Arts and Crafts influence. Filigree and wire wrapped jewelry are common, although their popularity wanes around 1910. White metals like silver and platinum are more popular than gold, but gold jewelry was still made and worn throughout the period.

Pavé-set gemstones compliment the continued popularity of invisible settings and the gypsy setting which first appears in the late 1870s is still a common setting style throughout the era. Jewelry is of course still prong set in both the coronet style and the Tiffany setting for diamonds.

# Chapter 6
# Art Deco
# 1917 to 1945

## Historical Background

Technology introduced in the early 20<sup>th</sup> century was part of the inspiration for the Art Deco movement. The Wright brothers introduced the first successful, manned, motorized flight in 1907. Henry Ford brought mass-production to the automotive industry, making the automobile affordable for the average man.

Although silent movies make their first appearance in 1888, silent films like *Cleopatra*, played by Theda Bara in 1915, helped to stimulate demand in a movie-going audience. In the artistic world, Pablo Picasso's controversial painting, *Les Demoiselles d'Avignon* exhibited in 1907 marked the beginning of cubism. Perhaps inspired by Picasso, Léon Bakst created colorful, abstract sets for the Ballet Russe (Russian Ballet) production of *Cleopatra* In 1909, and Schéhérazade in 1910.

In the scientific community, Howard Carter first opens the tomb of Tuk-tankh-amen in 1922. The two dimension tomb drawings and hieroglyphics coupled with the prominent use of lapis, carnelian, and other brightly colored gem materials fell in step with the developing Art Deco themes. The world seemed alive with high-speed transportation, moving picture films, exotic destinations, and brilliant colors.

By 1925 the decorative arts community had captured this enthusiasm in the form of stylized, streamlined, colorful motifs that today is called Art Deco. The term was shorted from the name of the 1925 *Paris Exposition Des Arts Décoratifs*. It is with Art Deco that Pierre Cartier's jewelry designs surpassed his contemporaries.

Al Jolson brings African American Jazz music to popular culture with the first talking film, *The Jazz Singer*. The free, heady feeling was not to last when an unregulated stock market crashed in 1929. After the crash there were numerous regulations and programs developed to protect consumers, but the economy remained in what today is called *The Great Depression*.

The Federal government using President Franklin Roosevelt's *New Deal* instituted numerous projects to try to stimulate the economy with limited success. The 1939 World's Fair with its theme of progress was intended to give hope and promote economic growth. Roosevelt's attempts were viewed as compassionate making him a very popular president. His Scottish terrier, Fala became a popular motif in jewelry. His new deal policies met with limited success, as what really pulled us out of the Great Depression was our participation in World War Two.

# Fashion Influences

After World War One, ladies hemlines began to rise. Wartime conservation had convinced women to abandon corsets in favor of the step-in, a one-piece garment that served as both camisole and pettipants. For the first time, ladies dresses belted at the hips, or hung straight from the shoulders with no emphasis on the bust or waistline. The ultimate challenge was to get one's beads to hang straight from the neck to the waist. The cloche style hat suited newly bobbed hairstyles. Straight-sided fur collars and fur coats completed the look.

By 1930, the waist-line returns to its natural position, the skirts lengthen, and the overall daytime look is tailored.

Woman's World tailored fashions for 1934.

5434
5433
5458
5263
5411

1920s sleeveless sack dress, woman wearing long sautoir.

Pierre Cartier with his wife and daughter both in cloche hats with jabot pins, 1926.

TO DRESS EXTRAVAGANTLY IN WAR TIME IS WORSE THAN BAD FORM IT IS UNPATRIOTIC

World War One War Department poster promoting conservatism in dress.

# Popular Jewelry Styles and Forms

## Lingering Belle Époque

The delicate, lacy mountings than adorned women before 1920 continue in popularity to some extent until the early 1930s. Brooches are typically slightly longer than they are high. Platinum topped brooches were formed in endless combinations of circles, squares, and triangles, sparsely accented with a few gems or possibly a small cameo. La Vallières are still popular showing lingering elements of Art Nouveau and Arts and Crafts.

Harvest moon brooches, starbursts, wishbones and kewpie dolls can still be found in jewelry motifs of the early 1920s.

## Art Deco

Jewelry from the early Art Deco era has a distinctive look. Pierced or pierced-style mountings were usually done in platinum, white gold, green gold, or silver, although some yellow gold was still used. The ever popular bar pin becomes increasingly longer and thinner as the 1920s progress, often matching the calibré cut bracelets, also set primarily in white metal. In the mid 1930s, jewelry takes on larger proportions leaving the delicate Belle Époque influences behind as jewelry gets bigger and bolder in the years before World War Two.

By the end of World War One, China resolved its internal political issues and resumed exports to the United States and Europe. Good luck charms with Chinese characters start to appear in catalogs. They often have very rectilinear proportions, consistent with angular stylized Art Deco forms. By 1933, carved pendants in jade and other semi-precious gemstones with chrysanthemums and other Asian motifs are also popular.

The stock market crash dramatically affected the jewelry industry, but not exactly in the manner one would suspect. Since few could afford fine jewelry, Bakelite and glass became very popular. They could be made into inexpensive, big, bold, and bright forms in defiance of a world fraught with poverty. Designers like Coco Chanel picked up on the trend making faux jewelry fashionable.

## Art Deco Jewelry

Hatpins are very short, four to five inches long, sometimes with an ornament on both ends. They were more ornamental than functional.

Drops suspended from chain or narrow links are popular earrings in the 1920s and 1930s, emphasizing motion motifs of the Art Deco form.

The barrette makes an appearance, in the early 1920s, keeping "bobbed" hair dos in place over the ears.

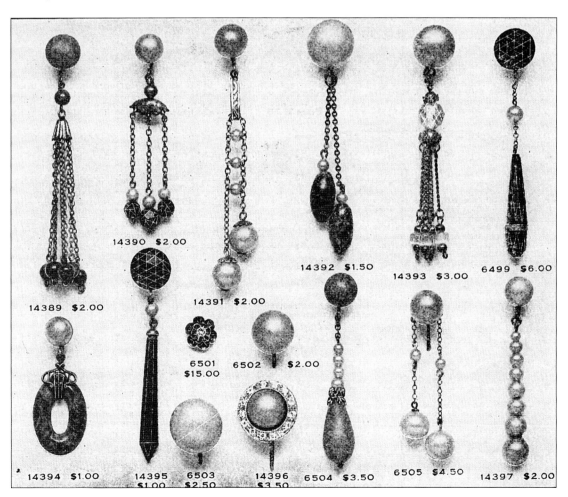

Drop earrings and stick pins from the 1922 Baird-North Catalog.

Ribbon necklaces continue in popularity. Graduated Bead necklaces and graduated pearl necklaces are popular throughout the Art Deco era. They ranged in length from 16 to 36 inches and were made in crystal and semi-precious gem materials. In the 1930s brilliant colored materials, including glass and Bakelite were commonly used in necklaces.

Brooches and Pendants had pierced metal fronts and gem accents. In the 1930s, etched crystal framed in white metal and accented with a diamond or paste were popular. They were sold individually and in sets that included combinations of bracelets, earrings, pendants, and brooches. Circle pins and stylized bowknots set with gems or pastes were also common design elements.

Sleeveless sack dresses created lingerie emergencies. The straps of the newly invented step-in undergarment would slip down onto bare shoulders. Small, rectangular, matching lingerie clips held the slip to the bra in a fashionably elegant way.

Dress clips and fur clips were in common use by 1930. Dress clips were sold in pairs and clipped at the corners of the necklace. For Bakelite dress clips, look for a clip assembly that is riveted or screwed in place, rather than glued. In 1927 Cartier patented a device that could hold two dress clips together so it could be worn with a brooch. Coro patented its costume jewelry version the "duette" in 1931. Fur clips had two prongs that plunged into fur collars popular at the time. Fur clips were sold individually, or sometimes with matching earrings.

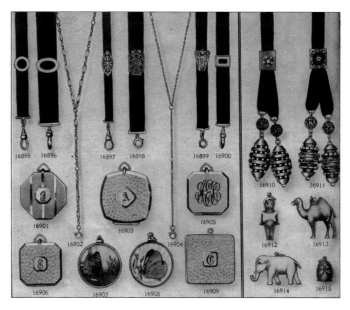

Ribbon Necklaces, lockets, and kewpie from 1922 Baird-North Catalog.

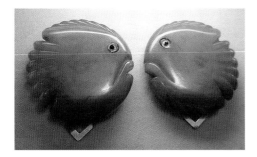

**Bakelite dress clips**, glass eyes, verso with riveted fitting.

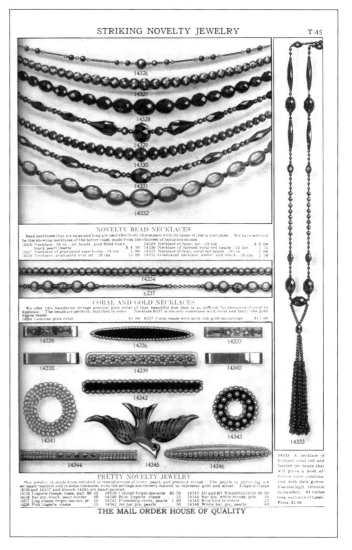

Bead necklaces and seed pearl brooches from the 1922 Baird North Catalog.

Bracelets take on a new look in the 1920s. Thin link bracelets feature either calibré cut stones, or delicate pierced metal, gradually widening in the 1930s. In the 1930s, bangle bracelets are set all around with gems or faux gemstones. Around 1925, bracelets with large alternating round and square links were sold as "slave bracelets". They could be set with gemstones or left with a plain metal surface. The 1933 Baird-North catalogue also advertised monogrammed ankle bracelets, worn under the stockings.

1920s bracelet in white gold and calibré cut sapphires. (Courtesy of Bélen Córdova).

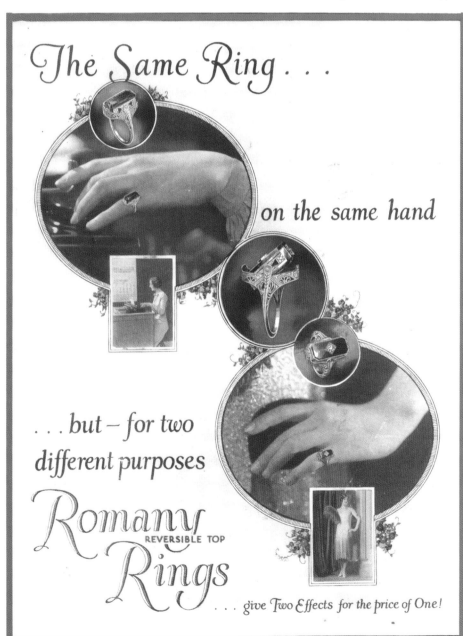

Advertisement for reversible rings, from 1925 A. C. Becken catalog

Rings were also set with gems all around, like bracelets. The first reversible ring is patented in 1925. One side featured a cameo that could be flipped over for a different look, usually onyx, set with a pearl or brilliant.

# Popular Gems and Gem Materials

In 1919 Marcel Tolkowsky introduced the brilliant cut diamond. It featured a wider table than the old European cut and it was not as deep. For the first time, the true brilliance of the diamond was displayed. This modern cut was the perfect compliment to modern themes expressed in the Art Deco style. Diamonds were used more than any other gemstone and in staggering quantities. Zircons and marcasites were popular substitutes for diamonds.

Sapphires and emeralds were next on the list of preferred gemstones. Opals, aquamarine, zircon, and topaz were also popular. Synthetic ruby and sapphire were both widely advertised, especially for use in rings.

Opaque and semi-opaque stones, like jade, lapis, chalcedony, and carnelian were used in pendants and earrings often with Asian motifs. Bead necklaces made with onyx, coral, and amber were popular gem materials for graduated bead necklaces.

Cultured pearls were much less expensive than natural pearls and were promoted actively by jewelers.

All of these gemstones could and were imitated in glass, Bakelite, and celluloid, especially after the stock market crash in 1929.

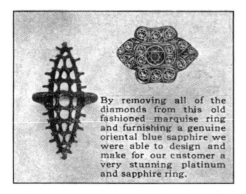

1922 Baird-North advertisement for remounting old gems in modern settings.

# Decorating, Finishing and Other Techniques

Jewelers widely promoted the idea of remaking old jewelry into new Art Deco forms and advertised the service in their retail catalogues. This explains the frequent occurrence of old European cut diamonds in Art Deco rings and brooches.

To survive the depression, many jewelers added less expensive lines of jewelry. Gold-filled, silver, and enameled jewelry was called "costume jewelry", though most of it was set with semi-precious gemstones. Many also adopted the practice of selling semi-precious gemstones, like garnet, in base-metal settings, reacquainting the consumer with a lesser quality of late Victorian style Bohemian garnet jewelry. Many jewelers stopped making fine jewelry altogether, and many did not survive the economic tragedies of the times.

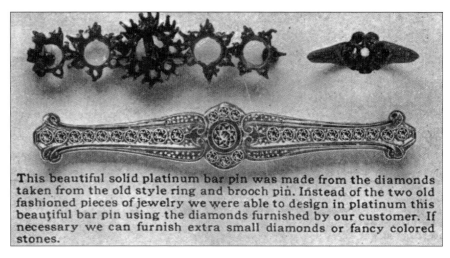

1922 Baird-North advertisement for remounting old gems in modern settings.

Chapter 7
# The Modern Era
### 1940 - 1960

## Historical Background

With the onset of World War II, peacetime factories in the United States that had been producing products for commerce were converted to produce products for the war effort. 16 million men served in the military, leaving women to fill their positions in the work force. Norman Rockwell glorified this new breed of woman with his 1943 magazine cover of "Rosie the Riveter". Conversion factories learned new techniques of mass production, many of which continued to be used in the years after the war was over. Everyone was expected to conserve. Food, gas, metals, and clothing were rationed. They were all needed for the war effort.

The atom bombs dropped over Hiroshima and Nagasaki were the most powerful weapons the world had yet to experience with the radius of immediate destruction of about one mile. When the war was over, close to 70 million people had lost their lives. Those who were fortunate enough to come home were anxious to put wartime memories behind them.

In the United States, a post-war effort was launched to get Rosie the Riveter out of the factory and back into the home, raising a family. Soon after the men came home, the baby boom began, lasting more or less officially until 1959.

1942 **War Department photograph** of a female riveter, working on the B-52 bomber.

# Fashion Influences

The sleek, tailored look of the late 1930s becomes the military look of the 1940s with padded shoulders and a-line skirts that gave women a little more freedom of movement. With the world returning to peacetime efforts of rebuilding those countries devastated by the war, clothing designers were quick to turn women's attentions away from factory jumpsuits and the short skirts that were the result of clothing rationing.

Christian Dior introduced his "new look" in 1947. He removed the wide, padded shoulders from women's jackets and created a tight-fitting bodice that flared at the hip. This was done to accommodate spacious full skirts and the return of the petticoat.

Women's suit jackets were worn fully buttoned. Form-fitting skirts had to have kick pleats to make it easier for ladies to walk in them. While the proportions of the skirted suit changed from the 1930s through the 1950s, there was one constant: jacket lapels that could accommodate brooches.

High school girls wore tight sweaters that buttoned up the front with full circle, poodle skirts, poodle pins and ponytails. The full skirt continues in popularity and in 1957 gets a new look in the form of the bubble skirt.

The era ends with Dior's introduction of the hobble skirt in 1959. It featured a loose fitting jacket, soft belted waistline and a tight skirt with the new length ending just above the knee.

Mamie Eisenhower wearing the new look in fashion, circa 1955.

# Popular Jewelry Styles and Forms

### Victorian Revival

The Victorian revival really began before World War II, interrupted by the troubles of a modern society. Victorian styles may have reminded women of a simpler, more gracious era, but the modern expression of it created a look that is distinctly different from the era it choose to copy. Mesh metal chokers were never worn during the Victorian era, but they are found in Victorian Revival jewelry. Victorian *Revival* adjustable bracelets usually have a large center stone and a matching pendant necklace, consistent with more bold style preferences of the 1940s and 1950s. Modern watch chatelaine/brooches also copied Victorian styles. The most common element seen is the brushed metal look or "Florentine" finish, as it takes its inspiration from the Etruscan Revival bloomed gold jewelry of the mid 19th century. In general, Victorian revival jewelry is much larger and bulkier than its Victorian counterparts.

1940s Victorian revival brooch by Art.

1940s Victorian revival brooch, probably by Robert.

## Mid-Century Modern

The aftermath of the atom bomb had a profound effect on the artistic community. A generation of young people nicknamed beatniks feared that total destruction was near and that they would not live to fulfill dreams of career and family. "Atomic" jewelry faintly resembled the structure on an atom. Sometimes the atom was designed like a snowflake.

The line between art and decorative art blurred as artists like Salvador Dali and Picasso experiment with jewelry as an art form. A new generation of jewelers bring abstract art to jewelry forms. Jewelers like Margaret de Patta explored the biomorphic style, creating abstract forms that are suggestive of organic forms. Abstract jewelry also took on architectural form, through artists like Ed Wiener. Sculpture Alexander Calder created jewelry versions of his mobiles combining geometric and abstract shapes.

Established jewelers like Boucheron picked up on the abstract trend creating their own versions of the abstract styles. Costume jewelers soon followed making commercialized versions of both studio and high fashion jewelers.

For the less adventurous, winding strips and folds of polished metal formed floral sprays brooches with pearl or jeweled accents. Bracelets and necklaces of tubes and balls took on the look of machinery.

1950s brooch with a snowflake motif.

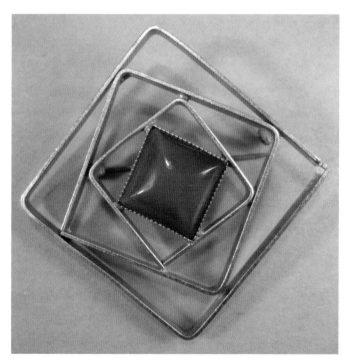

Mid-century modern brooch, West Germany.

Mid-century modern brooch, Norway.

### Romance, Novelty, and Whimsy

The war years brought new types of patriotic jewelry. Wire-wrapped letters spelled words like "mother" or "sister" and were worn by family and friends of military serving overseas. Brooches in red, white, and blue gave women a sense of patriotism. Women also wore military insignia brooches. They were much larger than their World War I counterparts, which were often less than half an inch in diameter.

After the war, an entirely different style of jewelry was popular in mainstream culture. Whimsical motifs with dancing ballerinas, wide-eyed, furred and feathered animals, sat daintily on lapels. Naturalistic motifs of flowers and butterflies were also very popular. For an added touch, some element could be mounted on a spring making cute dogs with bobbing heads and butterflies that appeared to flutter above a flower.

Since Coco Chanel made faux pearls an acceptable fashion accent, multi-strand, graduated faux pearl necklaces were widely marketed. Life imitated fiction as American women bought brightly colored and colorless rhinestone suites like they saw on their favorite actresses.

Dress clips and fur clips continued to be popular jewelry forms, taking on both abstract and traditional forms.

Chain link bracelets held charms commemorating trips, events, and hobbies. I.D. bracelets with monograms were popular gifts as were birthstone rings, both adding a personal touch to gift giving.

Some studios, like Wendell August Forge, managed to combine elements of the mid-century modern style with romantic motifs, creating a style that was unique to their studio.

**Whimsical brooch** by Hattie Carnegie.

**World War Two "Sweetheart" Brooch**, navy insignia, with a World War One "In Service" pin.

# Popular Gems and Gem Materials

Diamonds or anything that vaguely resembled diamonds were popular in fine jewelry throughout the period. Rubies, sapphires, aquamarine, and pearls were staples.

Studio jewelers often used no gemstones at all. Some used semi-precious cabochon cuts, and some used "found material" which could be any material that could complete the desired look.

For the budget conscious, rhinestones were reasonable substitutes. They were liberally employed. The best rhinestones were made of lead crystal giving them more brilliance. Foil backing made less expensive rhinestones look brighter. Lucite, a new plastic that was clear and did not yellow, was widely used in costume jewelry. Opaque plastics could be used to look like turquoise or coral, both popular semi-precious gemstones of the period. Enameled jewelry was used in all styles of jewelry, although its use in fine jewelry was limited.

# Decorating, Finishing and Other Techniques

Studio jewelers used a lot of non-precious metals including steel and copper. Much of it was made without any gemstones, relying on the interplay of the form against its background or the interplay between the piece and the wearer's clothing.

World War II production techniques taught many jewelers that back of a piece did not have to be finely cast, buffed and finished.

Metal shortages during World War II forced costume jewelers to use white base metal instead of traditional copper and brass. When the gold plating inevitably wore off, the silver showing through made the jewelry quickly unwearable. Most no longer used prong setting for rhinestones and other gem substitutes, choosing instead to glue-set. Less expensive designs were stamped out of sheet metal. When jewelry was cast, the back was intentionally left with a course pattern eliminating the need to hand finish the back.

**Back** of a 1940s brooch with a modern finishing technique.

## Jewelry Timeline: 1760-1960

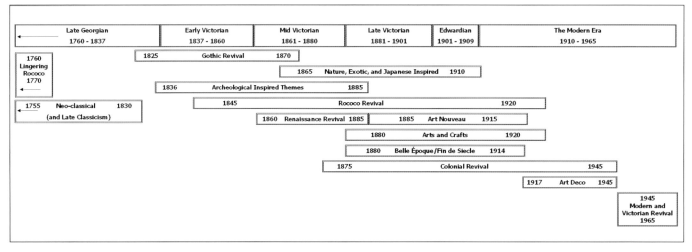

**Jewelry timeline** of periods and styles, 1760 to 1960.

# Chapter 8
# Gem Identification and Value Pointers

There are some simple identification tips that can be used to identify some gem materials used in jewelry. They do not require any special instruments other than a loupe, a black light, a penlight, a hot-point needle, and sight identification. Keep in mind that anything you apply to the surface of a gem or gem material should be done on the back or on an area that is not visible from the front. Also, try to use more than one identification method to make sure the results are accurate.

## Using a Loupe

### Finding Your Dominant Eye

One eye is your dominant eye. Usually, if you are right handed, your right eye is dominant and if you are left handed, your left eye is dominant. But there is a quick test. Point to an object across the room with both eyes open. Close your left eye. Does your finger appear to jump to one side? If the answer is yes, then your left eye is dominant. Try the same test with your right eye closed. If your finger appears to jump to one side, your right eye is dominant.

### Holding the Loupe at the Proper Distance

You will hold the loupe to your dominant eye keeping both eyes open. This is very important because you will strain your eye if you don't keep both eyes open. It's a little strange at first, but pretty easy to do with some practice.

Next, while holding the loupe, rest your thumb on your cheekbone. The loupe should be about one inch away from your eye at this point.

### Bringing the Object into View

Finally, bring the object to the loupe. This is extremely important. Do not bring the loupe down to the object. Sometimes, you may need a little more light so try to move under a light source or just tilt your head back a bit. People make two mistakes when trying to use a loupe. They want to use it like a magnifying glass holding the loupe over the object but about a foot away from their eye. While you will see magnification, the "field of vision" is limited. You will see five to six times more surface area when you hold the loupe to your eye.

## General Testing Tips

### Using a Black Light

Some gems and gem materials will fluoresce with a small, long wave, black light. The way each substance reacts under black light will be different. The reactions are described below for each substance. Just remember that if you are seeing purple reflecting from the surface, that this is not fluorescence, it is purple light reflecting back to your eyes. Most portable or battery operated black lights that you can buy are long wave and not harmful, but try to avoid staring directly into the light. Short wave black light can harm your eyes. The tests used here are for long wave, not short wave black light.

### Testing with a Hot Point

Destructive testing (hot-point) is not generally recommended on any piece of jewelry. Instead trying using it on a sample so that you can develop a memory for the way it should smell. Then later you can use either hot water or rub your thumb on the piece until it feels slightly warm. If you must hot needle test, do it quickly on the back of the piece and leave as small a mark as possible.

### Hand Carving

A hand carved item will not show consistent depth to the line. The stroke will start shallow and possibly narrow, then widen and deepen as the stroke progresses. Stamped designs will look uniform, of equal width, and depth.

### Using the Tooth Test

Gemstones and glass are hard substances compared to things like plastic, ivory, bone, and rubber. While there are hardness points that you can buy, an easy test is to tap it on your tooth and listen to the sound of the tapping in your ears. Hard substances will have a high-pitched sound; soft substances will have a low-pitched sound. If you use this test, you have to use real teeth, not dentures or implants.

## Amber

Nicknamed "the gold of the north" amber has been used in jewelry for thousands of years. Amber is a fossilized resin from pine trees. Large reserves of amber have been found on the seabeds of the Baltic Ocean. Baltic Amber is found in 256 shades of yellow, red, brown, near white, blue-green, green, and lavender. Lavender amber is very rare.

There are two easy tests for amber. The first is hot-needle testing. It will have a pine scent. Also, since it is an organic material, it tends to hold the scent of perfumes. The other way to test amber is with a black light. Amber will turn an opaque milky yellow under a black light. One image shows pieces of amber under normal light. The other image shows the same pieces under fluorescent light.

Pieces of amber in normal lighting and under fluorescent lighting.

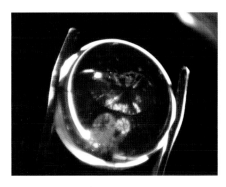

Heat-treated amber showing "lily pads".

Sometimes amber is heat-treated to clarify it, because it is considered to be more valuable. This may lessen the amount of fluorescence, but more importantly, heat-treating amber will create "heat spangles". They look like little lily pads and can be seen with a loupe.

If you have amber beads, you may also be able to see polish lines on the facet surfaces that would not be present in mold-formed plastic beads.

## Bakelite

Bakelite was invented in 1907 by Dr. Leo H. Baekeland. It is a phenol-formaldehyde product. It is a dense plastic that was used to imitate jet, ivory, bone, coral, and tortoiseshell. It was also used as a fun and colorful costume jewelry material that really didn't resemble anything but plastic. Early Bakelite bracelets were drawn out in long tubes (extruded) and cut off like donuts. Early designs were hand-cut. In either case, look for evidence of hand carving.

There are a couple of chemicals that have been effective in identifying Bakelite, *Formula 409*, a liquid, and *Happich Simichrome* a paste. Both will turn yellow when they come in contact with Bakelite. Simichrome is easier to carry around, as there is no chance of it leaking like Formula 409.

Bakelite also has the strong odor of formaldehyde. Dipping the piece in very hot water will release the formaldehyde odor. This works better than rubbing the surface with your thumb. Hot needle test at your own risk.

You can also use a black light to test Bakelite. It will have the same kind of opaque or milky fluorescence like amber. It is also very difficult to see fluorescence in white and very dark Bakelite so a second test will be necessary.

## Bog Oak

Bog oak comes from Ireland's bogs. Long exposure to water and elements made it darker and harder, thus a good material for carving. Commercial use of bog oak in jewelry began around 1845 and continued to be used throughout the 19th century, although not much is featured in catalogs after about 1880. Bog oak was hand carved until about 1852, at which time machine-stamped designs were used. They will not look as sharp as a hand carved piece. It will have a wood odor when tested with a hot point, but try rubbing the back first.

Since bog oak came from Ireland, it will almost always have an Irish motif like shamrocks, a hound, tower, or harp. There is an example in the price guide that is a carving of St. Patrick's cathedral in Armagh, Northern Ireland, completed in 1873.

## Bone

Bone is often confused with ivory because they will both usually show signs of carving. Bone is not as dense as ivory, so it cannot be polished to a smooth finish like ivory. It will have a course surface, partly due to the presence of Haversian canals, a system that transports blood cells to newly forming bones. They look like tiny lines or channels in the bone. For larger surfaces, try shinning a penlight through the piece. It will make them more visible. For smaller surfaces, like spacer beads, the course surface will be the best clue. When used with a hot needle bone will smell like burning hair.

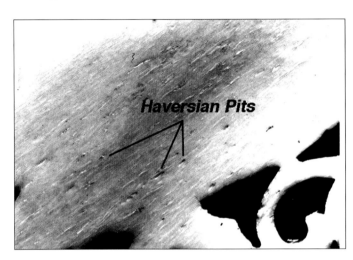

**Bone** at 10 times magnification showing Haversian canals.

## Cameos

A cameo can be defined as a carved, etched, or engraved design creating a relief or intaglio image in the gem or gem material in which it is carved. In the case of layered gemstones, the top color is cut away to reveal a second, and sometimes third color beneath. In practice, many other substances are used to make cameos, including glass, ceramics, micromosaics, lava, plastic, shell, ivory, and coral, The Romans even carved cameos out of turquoise. Cameos can be formed by bonding two substances together, as in the case of Wedgwood jasper cameos.

The value of a cameo is determined by many factors, a few of which are covered here. In general, all other things being equal, hard stone cameos sell for more than shell cameos. There are two easy ways to tell the difference. Since shells have curved surfaces, shell cameos are not flat. The curve can be viewed from the back of the cameo, or by looking at the bezel in which the cameo is mounted. The image shows how the height of the bezel changes to accommodate the curve of

a shell cameo. If the back of the cameo is visible, you may be able to see the curve of the shell.

Uneven bezel used to set a shell cameo.

If the cameo has an open back, hold it up to the light. Cameos damage easily and a strong light source will usually show cracks. A cracked cameo will sell for up to 70% less than one in good condition, so it is well worth the time to inspect it.

Since glass and plastic are used effectively to imitate hand carved cameos, use a loupe and check to see if you can find evidence of hand carving. The best place to look is at the areas where the bottom layer meets the top layer. You can also check for mold lines (see discussion on glass identification). To tell if your cameo is made of plastic or ivory, use the tooth test (discussed above).

New technology introduced in the late 20th century gave cameo carvers the ability to use lasers to cut cameos. Laser cameos can be very detailed. That is to their advantage, but the same cameo can be reproduced unlimited number of times making them little more than a mass-produced piece, rather than a single, unique piece of decorative art. Laser cameos are readily detectable by inspecting the surface around the portrait area. Instead of carving marks, there will be irregular dots or "snowflakes" for lack of a better word.

## Celluloid

Celluloid is a very early form of plastic and was used extensively in the 19th century. It was first developed and marketed for jewelry in 1876. Bakelite eventually replaced it, but there are many examples of early 20th century jewelry that use both. Celluloid was used to imitate coral, bone, ivory, and tortoise. Celluloid was mold-formed, often in two-piece molds that created a mold line at the seam. It was not hand-carved, so look for signs of carving. It does not fluoresce, so you can use a black light to distinguish it from both Bakelite and tortoise. Celluloid does not react to Formula 409 or Simichrome polish. When hot needle tested, celluloid smells like camphor.

Celluloid will often show lines that look a lot like those found in elephant and mammoth ivory. The lines are very obvious and can look like ivory, but they will not show cross graining like ivory. There can also be curving and swirls, something you would never see in ivory.

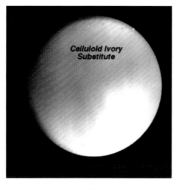

Celluloid drop with lines, with curving, but no reticulation.

## Coral

Coral comes in a variety of colors, including black, pink, salmon, white and red. The value is based on the size of the surface area (free of pits and imperfections) and the color with red coral being the most valuable, black being the least valuable. Small pieces of coral with a lot of surface imperfections were typically carved into small rosettes and leaves, and then mounted. Coral cameos are rare as large surface areas free of pits are not common. Much of the coral from the 19th century was harvested and carved in Naples, Italy.

Both plastic and glass were used to imitate coral. The tooth test is useful to separate coral from plastic. To determine if it is coral, look for evidence of carving and the lack of mold lines. Look for other defects found in molded glass. Finally, light will shine through glass, not coral.

## Diamonds

The cut of a diamond can help identify when a piece was made. For the late Georgian period through the 20th century, there are four cuts that are important, the rose-cut, the old mine-cut, the old European cut, and the modern brilliant cut. Since diamond is the hardest substance, early cutters did not have the ability to cut round diamonds. They also did not understand the theory of light. They thought that cutting facets in a diamond released the light; not knowing that it was the sun's rays actually entering the gem, then reflecting light back out.

The mine-cut diamond is not really round, but a square with rounded corners. It was used until the old European cut was introduced in 1891. The power bruiting machine allowed cutters to cut round diamonds. These cuts are often confused because both have deep pavilions and large culets.

When the modern brilliant cut was introduced in 1919, jewelers began using the new cut that gave diamonds the brilliance we see in them now. Many jewelers in the 1920s and 1930s advertised that they would set old diamonds in new style settings, so you will often find old European cut, mine-cuts, and even rose-cuts in Art Deco jewelry.

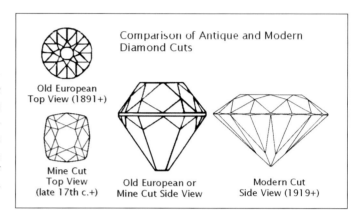

Comparison of Antique and Modern Diamond Cuts

Old European Top View (1891+)

Mine Cut Top View (late 17th c.+)

Old European or Mine Cut Side View

Modern Cut Side View (1919+)

Comparison of an old mine-cut, old European cut, and a modern brilliant cut.

Rose-cut diamonds are flat on the bottom with no table. They were usually used as accent stones, and they will be irregularly cut. If the cuts are too symmetrically precise, they may be 20th century reproductions designed to fool the consumer.

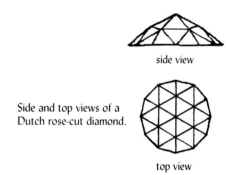

side view

Side and top views of a Dutch rose-cut diamond.

top view

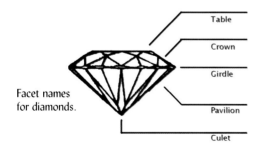

Table

Crown

Girdle

Pavilion

Culet

Facet names for diamonds.

## Glass

Glass is effectively used to imitate diamonds, colored gemstones, jet, onyx, coral, and turquoise to name a few materials. With a little practice, glass is an easy identification. Glass used in antique jewelry is formed in one or two-piece molds. When they are formed in two-piece molds, there will be a visible line where the mold pieces meet. If glass is formed to look like a faceted bead or gemstone, the edge where the facets meet will be rounded looking when viewed through a 10x loupe. Since glass is softer than most gem materials, those facet edges tend to chip in a ring-like pattern, referred to as a concoidal fracture. This should not be used a single identifying factor as there are gemstones that chip easily, too.

There are lots of things that happen when hot glass is poured into molds. Gas bubbles form inside. As the glass cools it shrinks away from the mold, sometimes leaving marks called "orange peel" on the surface. One image shows orange peel on the underside of the hatpin. Other mold marks include crizzling (a rippling effect on the surface), and straw marks (short straight lines that score the surface). The other image shows straw marks.

"Orange Peel" surface on the back of a glass hat pin.

Straw marks on the back of a glass hat pin.

## Gutta Percha

Gutta percha is processed sap of a tree found in the Malayan Archipelago. It was originally imported from Calcutta in 1840, but commercial use began around 1855. Gutta percha has a faint plastic odor when a hot needle is used; it does *not* smell like rubber. Gutta percha is still used for root canals. Your can buy a small stick of it from your dentist for a dollar or so. There is a common misconception that gutta percha is unstable when exposed to the air for long periods. If you ask your dentist how long he has had those sticks sitting around, you will see that this is not the case. While is does dry out over time, there is still antique jewelry that uses gutta percha.

## Horn

Horn is often mistaken for tortoise shell. In its natural state, horn is a translucent, pale yellow material that will usually have a brown stripe running through it. This makes it easy to tell the difference between horn and tortoise, which has a mottled surface. Both are very pliable when heated. Horn was frequently pressed into molds to create decorative elements for jewelry. It was also often dyed black, making it difficult to tell the difference between horn, jet, gutta percha, and vulcanite.

The easiest test to tell the difference between dyed horn and opaque black materials is by shining a penlight through the surface. If it is molded and thick, try shining the light at the edges.

Both horn and tortoise fluoresce with a black light (see fluorescence under tortoise). The translucent areas become opaque, giving a pale, milky appearance.

When hot needle tested, horn smells like burnt hair.

## Ivory

Ivory comes from several sources, including narwhal, walrus, elephant and woolly mammoth. Ivory grows much like the rings of a tree, growing longer and thicker as the animal ages. Growth rings, referred to as reticulation, form a crosshatch pattern when cut across the grain.

Ivory cabochon showing reticulation.

The lines themselves are referred to as Schreger lines. The Schreger lines in elephant ivory intersect at an angle that is

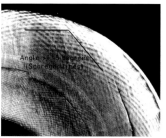

Schreger lines in elephant ivory, greater than 115 degrees.

Schreger lines in mammoth ivory, less than 90 degrees.

greater than 115 degrees. Schreger lines in mammoth ivory intersect at angles of less than 90 degrees. They are best observed at curved surfaces. The woolly mammoth is extinct, of course, but a large discovery of mammoth ivory was discovered in Siberia around 1872, so both elephant ivory and mammoth ivory were used in antique jewelry. Ivory was harvested from other animals, but the growth patterns differ in other animals. Only elephant and mammoth ivory show Schreger lines.

Ivory will have a much smoother surface than bone. Another way to tell the difference between ivory and plastic is to look for evidence of carving. There should not be any mold lines.

## Jet

Jet is fossilized coal and can be polished to a high gloss. It is very lightweight and when polished looks a lot like plastic. There were two sources of jet in the 18th and 19th century, Spain and Whitby, England. Spanish jet is softer than English jet and does not polish to a high gloss. The softer, Spanish jet did not hold detail as well as Whitby jet. In the Victorian era, jet was carved, polished, and mounted in jewelry primarily for mourning. Labor saving craftsmen did not polish unexposed surfaces or the crevices of carved areas. When carefully inspected, jet will be dull in these areas, plastic will be shiny. Since jet is carved by hand, look for evidence of carving or irregularity in the shapes. The image shows five pieces of jet from a bracelet. Notice the variation in the width and height of each piece. Had these pieces come from a plastic mold, they would have been uniform in size. There are two pieces at the top, sitting on their sides. The two pieces at the top of the photo are resting on their edges. These edges would not be visible when the bracelet was assembled and so have a dull appearance because they were not polished.

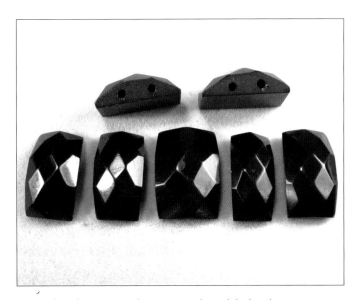

Pieces of jet showing irregular carving and unpolished surfaces.

## Pearls

There are entire classes taught about pearls, so the comments here will be understandably brief with a focus on telling the difference between real pearls, whether cultured or natural, and faux pearls (*faux* sounds better than *fake*.) The modern cultured pearl was not marketed until around 1905. This can act as act as a dating clue for antique and vintage jewelry since the benefit of cultured pearls is that if everything goes well they can be very round. Natural pearls are rarely round. This can help date a piece of antique jewelry or at least indicate if any of the pearls may have been replaced.

Both cultured pearls and natural pearls will fluoresce with a black light. They will look bright compared to faux pearls. The best way to test this is to use a strand that you know is either real or fake so that you have a result with which you can make a comparison. The images are examples of two strands of pearls. The strand on the right is real. On rare occasions, manufacturers of faux pearls use a bead that will fluoresce with a black light, so it's best to use a second test to confirm the results.

The the tooth test is fast and easy. Rub the pearl against your tooth; it will feel gritty. Faux pearls will feel smooth.

Faux pearls (left) and cultured pearls (right) under normal light and under fluorescent light.

## Synthetic Ruby

Synthetic ruby was used in jewelry since the late Victorian era. The early process produced streams of bubbles, so a thorough look with a loupe is very helpful. Synthetic rubies also fluoresce with a black light. One image shows a synthetic ruby in normal light. The other image shows the same synthetic ruby under fluorescent lighting. Synthetic rubies seem to light up and glow a bright red. While natural rubies can show mild fluorescence, it is not as extreme as with synthetic ruby, and will actually not be easy for the novice to detect.

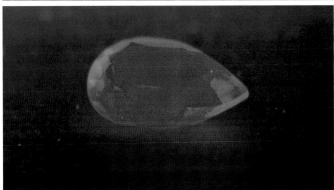

Synthetic ruby under normal light and under fluorescent light.

## Synthetic Sapphire

Both synthetic ruby and sapphire are formed in small containers about the size of a human thumb. The resulting gem material is called a boule. In the forming process melted powder drips down into the container with a slight curve forming curved color banding in the gem. These curved *striations* and curved color banding can be observed with a loupe. *Natural* Sapphire will frequently show straight color banding, an indication of natural origin.

## Tortoise

The shell of the sea tortoise has been used in toilette articles from the 16th century. Tortoise has a translucent, brown and pale yellow, mottled surface. Early artisans learned to inlay bits of metal and ivory into the surface of the shell. The most well known process is called piqué. It was not used in jewelry until the early 19th century. Fine examples usually date from the 1850s to the 1870s, with crude commercial production continuing into the early 20th century.

Tortoise and horn are very similar, so the tests that are positive for tortoise, like fluorescence, could mean the piece is made of horn, too. The translucent, pale yellow areas of tortoise will become opaque. Both horn and tortoise smell like burning hair with a hot needle test. If the piece is dyed black, it is probably made of horn. The mottled surface means it is tortoise.

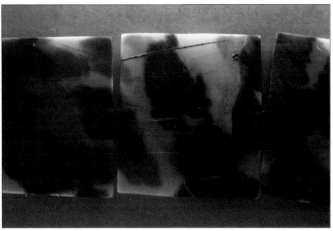

Tortoise shell under normal light and under fluorescent light.

## Union Case

Union Case was made by combining shellac and ground wood fiber. It has a glossy finish and is usually black. It was commonly molded to make cases for daguerreotypes and later dresser sets. There was some union case used for jewelry, mainly pressed into molds for decorative elements like bouquets of flowers. Over the years, union case can develop crazing, a fine web-like cracking on the surface, usually visible from the back.

## Vulcanite

Vulcanite is a black material made from vulcanized rubber. Charles Goodyear introduced the process in 1849. Among other things, it was used in jewelry and buttons. Vulcanite is easy to identify. Rub the surface of the piece until it feels slightly warm, and then smell it. It will smell just like automotive tire rubber. Over the years, vulcanite tends to fade becoming a yellowish brown.

# Chapter 9
# Metals, Fittings, and Findings in Jewelry

Gold and Silver were scarce and valuable metals in the 18th and 19th centuries. Many countries taxed jewelers based on the amount of gold and silver used in their pieces. There are a few dates that are useful in circa dating antique and vintage jewelry.

In the late Georgian era, it was common to set diamonds in silver, and colored gemstones in gold. It is common to find a late Georgian piece of jewelry made of gold and silver if the piece contains both diamonds and colored gemstones.

Rolled gold is a process of joining a thin sheet of gold to a sheet of base metal using pressure and heat from the friction of rolling to fuse the metals. It was used in jewelry from about 1817.

The invention of electroplated silver in 1840 and electroplated gold in 1844 allowed jewelers to use a very thin layer of precious metal for jewelry with base metal inside. Silver plated jewelry generally used a white base metal; gold plated jewelry used copper or copper alloys like brass or bronze for the base metal. The image shows the back of a hatpin where the copper base metal is visible between the gold gilding.

Manufacturers soon sought ways to reduce the amount of precious metal used in rolled gold and introduced *gold filled* jewelry. Gold filled jewelry differs from rolled gold jewelry. Much less gold was used, but in order to keep the bond between the copper and the gold, lead solder was introduced between the two layers of metal. This explains the dark gray spots that appear in Victorian jewelry when the gold wears down.

During World War II, many metals were rationed, especially copper and copper alloys. Manufactures switched to silver colored base metals under the electroplated surface, even for gold electroplating. The practice continues today with silver spots showing at wear points.

Back of a hat pin showing gilt metal and copper base metal.

Back of a gold-filled bracelet showing gray solder.

Another way to circa date jewelry is by the fittings and findings used by manufactures. Fittings are the *original* clips, clasp, hooks, pin stems, and hinges used to fasten jewelry to either the wearer or their clothing. Findings are later additions or repairs. The charts show fittings for earrings and brooches, and an example of what to look for in a repair. Used with popular styles and materials of the time should help to identify the time in which the jewelry was made. If you have a piece of jewelry that needs to be repaired, be sure to use a period finding. That is, do not add a modern safety clasp if the piece originally had a "C" clasp.

Condition is an important factor in valuing antique and vintage jewelry. Repairs to jewelry do affect value. Repairs or damage to the front of a piece will affect value more that damage or repairs to the back. Even slight damage, loss, or minor repairs visible from the front can affect the value as much as 80 percent. Extensive damage can take away the entire value. Repairs and damage to the back of the piece will also decrease the value, up to 40%, sometimes higher.

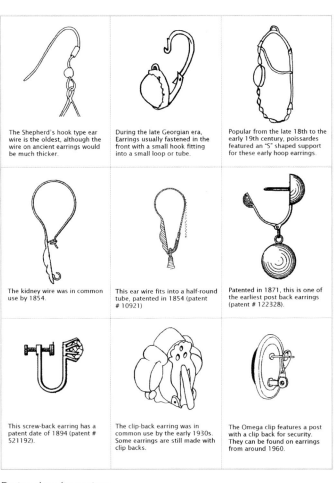

The Shepherd's hook type ear wire is the oldest, although the wire on ancient earrings would be much thicker.

During the late Georgian era, Earrings usually fastened in the front with a small hook fitting into a small loop or tube.

Popular from the late 18th to the early 19th century, poissardes featured an "S" shaped support for these early hoop earrings.

The kidney wire was in common use by 1854.

This ear wire fits into a half-round tube, patented in 1854 (patent # 10921)

Patented in 1871, this is one of the earliest post back earrings (patent # 122328).

This screw-back earring has a patent date of 1894 (patent # 521192).

The clip-back earring was in common use by the early 1930s. Some earrings are still made with clip backs.

The Omega clip features a post with a clip back for security. They can be found on earrings from around 1960.

Dating clues for earrings.

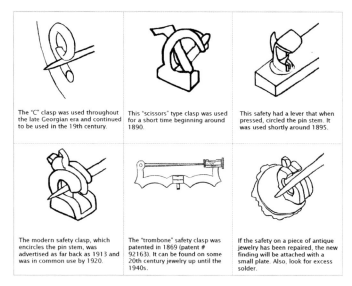

The "C" clasp was used throughout the late Georgian era and continued to be used in the 19th century.

This "scissors" type clasp was used for a short time beginning around 1890.

This safety had a lever that when pressed, circled the pin stem. It was used shortly around 1895.

The modern safety clasp, which encircles the pin stem, was advertised as far back as 1913 and was in common use by 1920.

The "trombone" safety clasp was patented in 1869 (patent # 92163). It can be found on some 20th century jewelry up until the 1940s.

If the safety on a piece of antique jewelry has been repaired, the new finding will be attached with a small plate. Also, look for excess solder.

Dating clues for brooch fastenings.

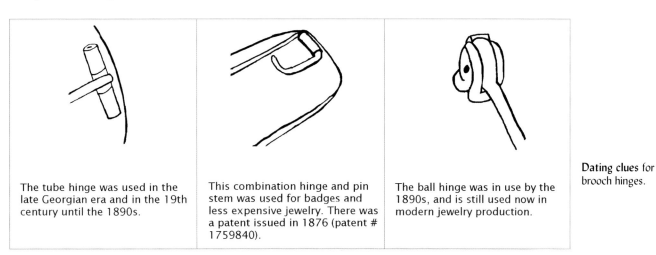

The tube hinge was used in the late Georgian era and in the 19th century until the 1890s.

This combination hinge and pin stem was used for badges and less expensive jewelry. There was a patent issued in 1876 (patent # 1759840).

The ball hinge was in use by the 1890s, and is still used now in modern jewelry production.

Dating clues for brooch hinges.

# Chapter 10
# Marks on Jewelry

Most countries have some sort of system for making sure that the content of the gold and silver is represented truthfully. Not only do different countries have different ways of marking gold and silver, but most countries' systems changed over the centuries. Some countries enforced precious metal marking laws and some did not. The result is that we can use assay marks to help us date antique and vintage jewelry.

Gold is typically measured in karat weight with 24 karats being 100% gold. The chart shown gives karat weights along with the percentage of gold and alloy.

| Gold Karat Measurement | | | |
|---|---|---|---|
| Karat | %Gold | %Alloy | Fineness |
| 24K | 100.00 | None | 1000 |
| 22K | 95.83 | 4.17 | 958 |
| 18K | 75.00 | 25.00 | 750 |
| 15K | 62.50 | 37.50 | 625 |
| 14K | 58.33 | 41.67 | 583 |
| 10K | 41.67 | 58.33 | 417 |
| 9K | 37.50 | 62.50 | 375 |

Table of gold fineness.

Silver is measured in *fineness*, with 1000 parts being pure silver. Sterling is 925 parts silver and 25 parts alloy.

In the 18th and 19th centuries, maker's marks are not common on jewelry. In countries like the Great Britain and France, makers were required to add their initials when a piece was hallmarked, but many jewelry items were too small to have hallmarks placed on them, leaving a large percentage of them either without maker's marks or with marks too small to identify.

In the United States hallmarking laws were left up to the individual states until 1906. The practice of adding a maker's mark became more common after 1881 when the Federal Government passed a law allowing and projecting individual trademarks. As a result, even rolled gold jewelry may contain maker's marks.

Very little costume jewelry is marked before World War II. For the collector of costume jewelry, this can affect value dramatically, with unmarked pieces selling for up to two-thirds less than a comparable marked piece. The quality of much costume jewelry has declined since the end of the 1950s. That is part of what makes it collectible. Many popularly collected manufactures produced some very poorly made jewelry before they went out of business, making how the piece is made just as important as who made it.

The name on a piece of jewelry then is about the reputation of the manufacturer. They have a reputation because of quality of design, quality of materials used, workmanship, and innovation. Use the maker's mark as a guide to selecting or valuing antique and collectible jewelry.

Manufacturers are listed by their complete business name. That means that Alexander Fisher is listed alphabetically by his first name, not his last.

The date(s) directly under the mark are for know dates of use for that mark. The dates in parenthesis are the known birth ("b") and death ("d") dates for the designer or the known dates that the company was in business.

# Maker's marks A to C.

1893 - 1896
(b.1864 - d.1936)

ALICE CAVINESS
(Post WWII - current)

ART©
(Post WWII - 1960s)

BALLE 925S STERLING NORWAY
1925+

Boucheron
1890
(1858 - current)

BOUCHERON
1978 - current

BVLGARI
1984
(1905 - current)

THE CARENCE CRAFTERS
Either mark or both marks found on jewelry
(1908 - about 1918)

CG — Carlos Giuliano
(1874 - 1914)

Cartier
1944
(1847 - current)

1971

1976

Cartier
Current

 Castellani
(1816 - 1930)

1988
(1920s - current)

CHANEL
2005

 Christian Dior
1947c
(1947 - current)

1989 (costume jewelry)

CINER
1949+
(1892 - 1931: fine jewelry)
(1931 - current: costume jewelry)

# Maker's marks C to H.

Coro
1920
(Cohn & Rosenberger: 1896 - 1979)

Andrée
1937

Coro Craft
1941

 Coro
1945

Cellini
1952

FUTURAMA
1954

Jewelcraft
1955

 WITCH
1904
(Daniel Low & Co: 1867 - 1990s)

D. ANDERSEN CHRISTIANIA
1876 - 1888
(1876 - current)

830 S
1888 - 1925

STERLING NORWAY
c1925+

DAVID-ANDERSEN NORWAY STERLING 925 S
c1925+

OAKES — Edward Everett Oakes
(b.1891 - d.1960)

ФАБЕРЖЕ
(Peter Carl Fabergé & Fabergé Cie: 1870 - 1920s)

Fabergé
1943
(Fabergé, USA)

FABERGÉ
1952

FABERGÉ
1981

FABERGÉ
Current

Florenza
1956 - c1962
(1955 - 1960s)

Florenza
1963

FLORENZA©

FROMENT MEURICE
1844
(François-Desire Froment-Meurice: b.1802 - d.1855)
(Emile Froment-Meurice: b.1837 - d 1913)

Goldette
1959
(1958 - 1970s)

 HW
HARRY WINSTON
Current
(b.1896 - d.1978)

Hattie Carnegie
1938
(1919 - 1970s)

Hattie Carnegie
1953 - 1956

Hattie Carnegie
1956+

DRÉGA
1965

# Maker's marks H to T.

Hobé
1926
(1880'S - current: fine jewelry)
(1926 - current: costume jewelry)

Hobé
1979

Hobé

1903 - 1917 / 1918 - 1932 / 1933 - 1957 / 1957 - 1983

HAND WROUGHT STERLING KALO
1913+
(1900 - 1970)

1945+
(1945 - 2006)

KENNETH LANE
1989 - 1996
(1963 - current)

R. LALIQUE
1885 - 1945
(1885 - current)

LALIQUE
1945 - current

LEA STEIN
(1969 - 1981)

L & Co
(1899 - current)

©Matisse
1952 - 1964
(Renoir/Matisse: 1946 - 1964)

MAUBOUSSIN
(1927 - current)

McClelland Barclay
(B.1891 - d.1943)

 MERMOD & JACCARD JEWELRY CO.
1864 - 1905
(1864 - 1975)
(Mermod, Jaccard, and King: 1905 - 1975)

Ming's
(1940 - 1999)

MIRIAM HASKELL
(Miriam Haskell: 1924 - 1983)

Miriam Haskell
1987
(Haskell Jewels:1983 - current)

Nettie Rosenstein
(1930s - 1970s)

PERUZZI BOSTON
(Peruzzi Sisters: 1930 - 1981)

©Renoir
(1952 - 1964)

 TF
(Theodor Fahrner: b. 1868 - d.1928)

# Maker's marks T to W.

TIFFANY & CO.
1893+
(1842 - durrent)

TIFFANY &Co.
1905+

TIFFANY
1920+
(jewelry with no precious stones)

TIFFANY & CO.
1920+
(jewelry with precious stones)

1928+
(jewelry with no precious stones)

TIFFANY & CO. SCHLUMBERGER STUDIOS
1993+

 Tortolani
1950 - 1976
(1950 - 1976, then 2002 - current)

Tortolani
2002 - current, re-issue

 Jewels by TRIFARI
1947+
(1917 - current)

 STERLING 925 FINE
1904
(Unger Brothers: 1872 - 1914)

©VENDOME
(Subsidiary of Coro: 1944 - 1979)

Vendôme
1956+

WEISS
(1942 - 1971)

WEISSCO
1948+

Weiss
1960 - 1962

AWLo
1962+

WENDELL AUGUST FORGE
(1923 - current)

1931 - 1933, impressed mark
(William Spratling: b.1900 - d.1967)

1933 - 1938
raised circle

 SPRATLING MADE IN MEXICO
1940 - 1946
raised irregular letters

# Canada

The Gold and Silver Marking Act of 1906 set standards for marking precious metals. The law also regulated imports into Canada. Imports bearing English hallmarks were exempt from Canadian marking requirements.

No item could be marked with the words gold, silver, sterling, or coin without showing the karat mark for gold or the fineness mark for silver. Gold was required to be marked in karats, such as 10k or 18k. Not only is Sterling defined as 0.925 fineness, but also words used like coin, coin silver, or silver must also be 0.925 fineness. Silver had to be marked with the fineness whether or not these words were used. No minimum standards were set for either gold or silver.

In 1934, Canada established a national mark consisting of a lion's head surrounded by a large letter "C". In 1978 the mark was changed to a maple leaf inside a large letter "C" and remains in effect today.

Manufactures who used any of these quality marks were also required to add the maker's initials or maker's trademark.

| Canadian National Mark 1934 to 1978 | Canadian National Mark 1978+ |

Canadian national marks.

The terms are listed along with acceptable abbreviations.

| Term | Abbreviation |
| --- | --- |
| Britannia Metal | B.M |
| German Silver | G.S. |
| Gold Electro Plate | Gilt |
| Gold Filled | G.F. |
| Nickel Silver | N.S. |
| Rolled Plate | R.P |
| Silver Electro Plate | E.P. |
| White Metal | W.M. |

**Canadian terms** for acceptable plated wares, 1906.

# France

After the French revolution, a new system of marking was adopted in France. This system applied to all of France, not just Paris and a few provinces. These marks formed the foundation for all later legislation. The system was changed again in 1838 and continues to be used to the present day with minor changes.

The 1838 system had five marks: the standard mark, the assay mark, the maker's mark, the verification mark, and the import mark. Gold and silver were assayed in Paris and in provinces outside of Paris (departments), each using their own symbol.

### The gold standard marks

There were actually three standards for gold in France, 0.920, 0.840, and 0.750. The head of a Greek physician was used for the standard mark with the number "1" by his forehead for the first standard of 0.920, assayed in Paris. The shape of the surrounding shield was an octagon. A symbol was placed under the chin for the departments.

### The second gold standard of 0.840 placed a "2" under his chin.

A barrel-shaped shield was used for the second standard. Symbols for the departments were placed behind the neck.

### The third standard, 0.750 placed a number "3" by his nose.

The shield was a hexagon. The department symbol was placed behind the neck.

In 1994, the French Government allowed for the assay of 14 karat and 9 carat gold.

The assay mark for Paris was the head of an eagle. The assay mark for the departments was a horse's head with the symbol for the department on the cheek.

| Table of French Punches in use from May 10, 1838 to January 1, 1962 | | |
| --- | --- | --- |
| Distinction | Paris and Departments | |
| Gold 1st Standard 0.920 | | Department symbol under the chin |
| Gold 2nd Standard 0.840 | | Department symbol behind the neck |
| Gold 3rd Standard 0.750 | | Department symbol behind the neck |
| Distinction | Paris | Departments |
| Gold Assay | | Department symbol on the cheek |

French gold marks, 1838 to 1962.

## The silver standard marks

There were two standards set for silver, 0.950 fineness and 0.800 fineness. The head of Minerva was used for the both standards, but the number "1" was used for the first standard and the number "2" was used for the second standard. The shape of the surrounding shield was an octagon for the first standard, and a barrel shaped shield for the second standard, the same shield shapes that were used for the gold standards. The department symbol was located under the chin for the first standard and in front of the forehead for the second standard.

### Table of French Punches in use from May 10, 1838 to January 1, 1962

| Distinction | Paris and Departments | |
|---|---|---|
| Silver 1st Standard 0.950 | | Department symbol under the chin |
| Silver 2nd Standard 0.800 | | Department symbol before the forehead |

| Distinction | Paris | Departments |
|---|---|---|
| Silver Assay | | Department symbol between the claws |

French silver marks, 1838 to 1962.

## The silver assay mark

The boar's head was used to show a Paris assay and the crab for the departments, each along with the symbol for the individual assay office already in use.

In 1962 the "Wild Boar's Head" mark that Paris used for its assay mark was replaced by the "Crab" mark already in use for the departments. The only difference was that Paris did not use a divisional mark.

In 1973, the French government changed the double silver standards of .950 and .800. From this point forward, a standard of .925 was introduced. The number one indicates the standard of .925 and is located at the *back* of Minerva's head (versus in front of Minerva's head before 1973). A letter under the chin indicates the decade beginning in 1973. The date letter for 1973 to 1982 is "A." The date letter for 1983 to 1992 is "B."

French silver mark, 1973+.

## The maker's mark

A kind of a flattened diamond called a "lozenge" was used for the maker's mark. The maker's initials were placed inside the lozenge. This symbol with initials is still used to identify the maker.

## The foreign guarantee mark

Gold and silver of foreign manufacture were tested for the minimum standard. The same mark was used for gold and silver, a weevil.

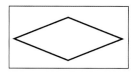

French maker's mark lozenge.

It was decided that any item marked before the new system took effect would simply be *verified* for content. It was called the *poinçon de recense*. The mark in use from 1838 was the head of a giraffe for small items and the head of a bulldog for large items. Watchcases were marked with a chimera. The symbol for the department was placed under the chin. No symbol was required for Paris.

### Foreign Guarantee, Verification and Assay Marks for Gold and Silver Punches in use from May 10, 1838 to January 1, 1962

| Distinction | Paris | Departments |
|---|---|---|
| Foreign Guarantee of minimum gold or silver standard | | Department symbol between the legs |
| Large Recense for gold and silver (Verification) of previous marks) | | Department symbol below the lower jaw |
| Small Recense for gold and silver (Verification) of previous marks) | | Department symbol on the collar |
| Assay for imported watches of minimum gold or silver standards | | Department symbol between the wings and back |

*The dotted lines shown by the guarantee marks, the verification mark and the watch assay mark indicate the shape of the punches for the Paris Assay Office only. Each department has a different symbol which is placed in the area of the dotted lines.

French foreign guarantee marks, 1838 to 1962.

## The import mark

Foreign items were not tested. They were marked with the letters "E" and "T" in a rectangle. Small foreign items were marked with a capital "E."

# Germany

The German states were unified in 1871. In 1888, new laws took effect for marking gold and silver. The maker's mark had to be registered at the Reichspatentamt. (Realm patent office) The maker's initials, along with the fineness in numbers had to be struck on the item by the manufacture. For gold, if the fineness was 580 or greater, the German crown enclosed in a circle was used. For silver, if the fineness was .800 or greater, the German crown and half-moon was added.

Goldsmiths could work at standards higher than those set for gold and silver. The item would then be marked with the fineness represented in thousandths.

German gold mark, 1888+.

German silver mark, 1888+.

# The United Kingdom

In 1238, King Henry III of England instituted the assay of gold and silver to prevent fraud. The law also prescribed that all items made of silver to be 925 parts silver to 75 parts copper, the same as the coin of the realm.

Over the next few hundred years, many laws were passed to control the quality of gold and silver. The result is that we can trace English gold and silver back to the year it was assayed by learning the basic marking system they used. A premium is placed on hallmarked English jewelry because of the ability to date a piece by reading those hallmarks.

In general, English gold and silver will have at least four marks, the quality mark, the town mark, the maker's mark and a date letter.

## The Gold Quality Mark

Originally, there was only one standard for English gold, 22 karat. In 1798, the 18-karat standard was added. In 1854, 15, 12 and 9-karat gold standards were added. In 1932, a 14-karat gold standard was added; the 15 and 12-karat standards were dropped. Today with the exception of Dublin, all of the assay offices use the same quality marks for gold.

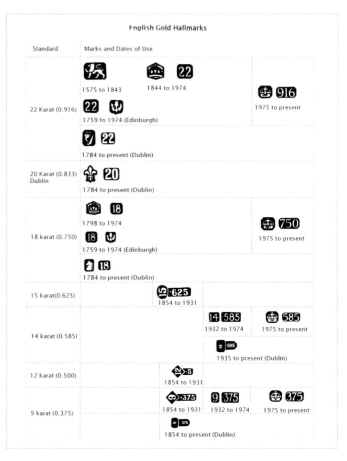
English gold hallmarks, 1575 to present.

## The Silver Quality Mark

Since 1720, there has been only one standard for English silver, 0.925 or Sterling. From 1549, a lion on all fours, called a lion passant, represented the Sterling standard. Edinburgh used a thistle and Dublin used Hibernia seated for their quality marks.

English Sterling silver marks.

## The Town Mark

There were many towns that assayed gold and silver. The majority of gold and silver was assayed in London, Sheffield, Birmingham, Edinburgh, and Dublin, although Sheffield did not assay gold until 1903. The current town marks for these offices are shown.

English town assay marks.

## The Maker's Mark

The maker's mark was required as early as 1327 in some towns. Most people were illiterate, so the maker's mark was usually a symbol. By 1720, when illiteracy was no longer a widespread issue, goldsmiths began using their initials to mark their wares.

## Date Mark

The date mark consists of a letter inside a shield. The individual assay offices varied slightly in procedure, but basically, a new letter was used for each year, beginning with "A" until the end of the alphabet was reached. London, for example, went in twenty-year cycles, excluded the letter J and stopping at "U" or "V." The font of the letters would change with each complete cycle, along with the shape of the shield. Sheffield went all the way to "Z" in the alphabet.

# The United States

As a British colony, America was intended to provide raw materials to Great Britain. In exchange, England would have an outlet for finished goods, including, jewelry, silver flatware and hollowware. As such, England never established assay offices in the American Colonies.

In fact, no legal system of marking precious metals was adopted in the United States until the National Metal Stamping Act of 1906. There are no assay offices in the United States.

For gold, the law established acceptable tolerances when the karat weight was placed on the piece.

For silver, this law required that if a piece of silver is marked with the words "sterling," it must be 0.925 fineness. If the piece is marked "coin," it must be 0.900 fineness. There is a common misconception that the United States stopped using coin silver after the civil war. The fact that the law provides for the use of the word "coin" implies that silversmiths continued to use the coin standard into the twentieth century.

The fact that the federal government waited so long to adopt these laws was a reflection on a basic constitutional issue, that of state's over federal government rights. Many states had already adopted laws governing the marking of precious metals. Most date back to the 1890s, which may explain why many 19th century items are clearly marked. Also, more reputable retailers and manufacturers used marking as a measure of their reputation and a way to indicate the quality of their items.

# SECTION TWO

# Chapter 11
# Estate Jewelry with Values Referenced

If there is a single thing that has affected jewelry prices in the past ten years, it would be the Internet. It is all about supply and demand. Much vintage jewelry once thought to be rare is in fact common; prices have gone down. Many Georgian pieces believed to be unobtainable can be purchased from all over the world, creating fierce bidding wars and high priced boutique web sites that specialize in their sale.

Because of the profound effect of the Internet on the prices for jewelry, the values set for the pieces in this price guide rely heavily on the influence of the Internet. Caution is advised as anyone with or without experience can offer items for sale on the Internet. An asking price is not necessarily a real price.

There are several Internet sources that list auction house prices from both the United States and Europe that were instrumental in setting retail values for the jewelry in this price guide. The benefit of using auction values to arrive at price is that this is actually what a dealer or collector paid for the jewelry at auction. By comparing actual sales at fair market value, retail asking prices that are too high or too low stand out immediately.

## Belts and Belt Buckles

**Belt Buckle**, late Victorian, 1880s, roses of dyed and molded horn, each is 2.5 in. high. Value $75

**Belt Buckle**, late Victorian, butterfly, cut-steel, 2.375 in. high. (Courtesy of Lisa L. Olson). Value $75

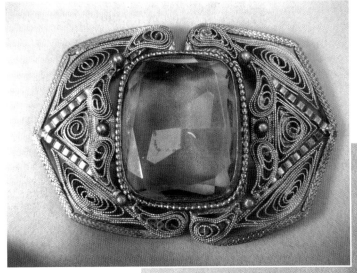

**Belt Buckle**, late Victorian, 1880s, blue glass, brass filigree, 3 in. wide. (Collection of Barbara Seaman). Value $65

**Belt Buckle**, Art Deco, 1917 – 1930s, geometric shapes in Bakelite, overall length of 3.875 in. wide. Value $75

**Belt Buckle**, Art Deco, marked "patent no 1965116", (1934), black Bakelite, overall wide of 3.125 in. (Author's Collection). Value $75

**Belt**, Mid-Century Modern, Wendell August Forge, 1940s – 1950s, roses of hand-hammered aluminum, 46 in. long. (Courtesy of Joy Ste. Marie). Value $90

# Bracelets

**Bracelet**, early Victorian, 1840s – 1850s, expandable woven hair with photo compartment, rolled gold, safety chain, 6 in long. (Collection of M.Q. Iacovetti). Value $450

**Bracelet**, early Victorian, 1830s – 1860, gold-filled, knot motif with central citrine colored glass, woven and braided hair, 8 in. long. (Courtesy of Roberta Knauer Mullings, G.G.). Value $350

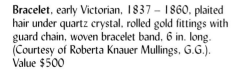

**Bracelet**, early Victorian, 1837 – 1860, plaited hair under quartz crystal, rolled gold fittings with guard chain, woven bracelet band, 6 in. long. (Courtesy of Roberta Knauer Mullings, G.G.). Value $500

**Bracelet**, mid-Victorian, Etruscan Revival bypass, c1870, rolled gold, 2.25 in. diameter. (Courtesy of finderskeepersvintage.com). Value $275

**Bracelet**, mid-Victorian, 1870 – 1880s, snake's heads, silver-plated, bypass with snakeheads are each 0.625 in high, bracelet is 2.37 in. diameter. (Author's Collection). Value $175

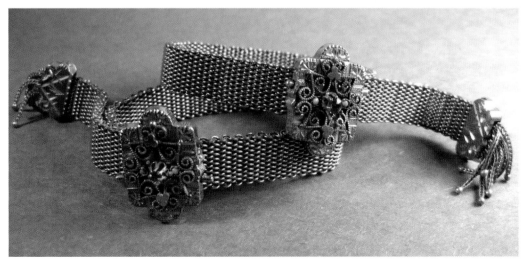

**Mesh Bracelets** (2) mid-Victorian, 1870s – 1880s, shield-shaped slides set with faux turquoise and paste, mesh bands with pelleted tasssels, rolled gold, each is 9.5 in. long. (Author's Collection). Value $600

**Bracelet**, mid-Victorian, 1860 – 1870s, lion's head, ruby eyes, holding a diamond in his mouth, 14 karat. (Courtesy of Ebert and Company). Value $1,500

**Bracelets** (2), mid-Victorian, Renaissance Revival bypass style, manufacturer's date of 1882, rolled gold, channel-set garnets glass, 2.25 in. diameter. (Collection of Heather Gates). Value $295

**Bracelets** (2), mid-Victorian, bangle bracelets with buckle motif, rolled gold, 3 in. diameter. (Collection of Heather Gates). Value $335

Bracelet, mid-Victorian, Etruscan Revival, 1870 – 1880, bypass with rose-cut garnets, rolled gold, 2.25 in. diameter. (Collection of M.Q. Iacovetti). Value $375

Bracelet, mid-Victorian, patent date of 1879, bypass, rolled gold bangle bracelet set with a hard-stone cameo, 2.0625 in. diameter. (Courtesy of Roberta Knauer Mullings, G.G.). Value $265

Bracelet, mid-Victorian, patent date of 1879, bypass enameled bangle with a painted glass portrait of a Japanese deity, 2 in. diameter. (Courtesy of Roberta Knauer Mullings, G.G.). Value $275

Bracelet, mid-Victorian, 1870s – 1880s, roses in bright orange celluloid, 2 in. wide. (Courtesy of Lisa L. Olson). Value $120

**Bracelet**, Arts & Crafts, late 19th century, marked "Gorham Pewter", 0.937 in high, 2.625 in. diameter. (Author's Collection). Value $195

**Bracelet**, Arts & Crafts, band marked "chrome", c1900, horn, hand carved and dyed, paste and bead accents, face is 1.5 in. diameter. (Courtesy of Diana Miller, Out of the Attic). Value $120

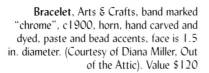

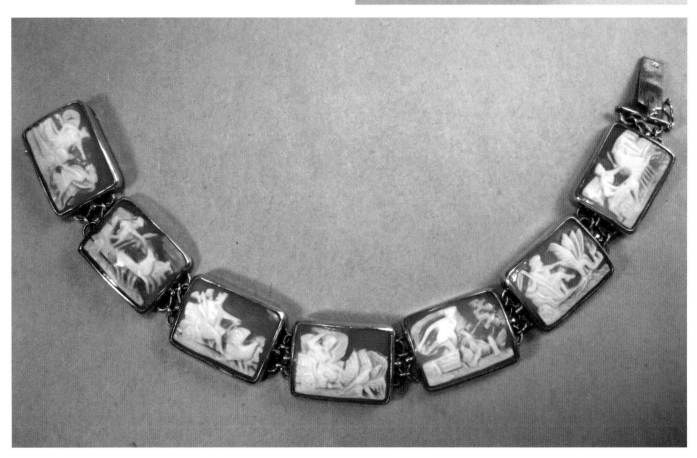

**Bracelet**, late Victorian, 1880s, marked "16k", shell cameos depicting Greek Gods in a chariot race, gold mounting, 6.75 in. long. (Courtesy of finderskeepersvintage.com). Value $1,425

**Bracelet**, late Victorian, 1880s – 1890s, hinged bangle engraved with flowers and foliage, rolled gold, 3 in. diameter. (Collection of M.Q. Iacovetti). Value $250

**Bracelet**, late Victorian, Birmingham Hallmarks for 1895, turquoise, natural pearl, 9 karat gold, 2.75 in. diameter. (Collection of M.Q. Iacovetti). Value $475

**Bracelet**, late Victorian, 1880s, heart motif of turquoise, natural pearl, rolled gold, 2.75 in. diameter. (Collection of M.Q. Iacovetti). Value $375

**Bracelet**, late Victorian, dove with an olive branch, rolled gold, stamped "S & W", 2.75 in diameter. (Courtesy of Roberta Knauer Mullings, G.G.). Value $175

**Bracelet**, late Victorian, 1890s – 1900, sapphire, fresh water pearl, rose gold, hinged with safety chain, 3 in. diameter. (Courtesy of Lisa L. Olson). Value $425

**Bracelet**, late Victorian, 1880s, 14k gold-filled, woven mesh set with an old European cut diamond, approximately 0.0355 ct, 6.75 in long. (Collection of Debbie White). Value $200

**Bracelet**, Art Nouveau, cinnabar and brass, 7.75 in long. (Courtesy of Roberta Knauer Mullings, G.G.). Value $140

**Bracelet**, Edwardian, c1905, hinged bangle engraved with flowers, interior inscribed "Dec 25 07", rolled gold, 3 in. diameter. (Collection of M.Q. Iacovetti). Value $175

**Bracelet**, Belle Époque, 1920s – 1930s, 5 graduated shell cameos, gold-filled links, 7 in. long. (Courtesy of Roberta Knauer Mullings, G.G.). Value $400

Bracelet, Belle Époque, 1920s – 1930s, 9 graduated shell cameos, silver links, marked "800", 7.25 in. long. (Courtesy of Roberta Knauer Mullings, G.G.). Value $425

Bracelet, Art Deco, 1925 – 1935, large gem-cut, multi-colored pastes, serrated brass spacers, on chain, 8 in. long. (Courtesy of Diana Miller, Out of the Attic). Value $75

Bracelet, 1917 – 1918, "In Service", patriotic motif, ribbon bracelet is 7 in. long; pendant portion is 0.75 in. long. (Courtesy of Lisa L. Olson). Value $85

**Bracelet**, marked "silver" and "Italy", 1920s – 1930s. roses and geometric shapes in micromosaics, tesserae are red, white, and blue, 7.125 in. long. (Courtesy of Lisa L. Olson). Value $165

**Bracelet**, 1920s – 1930s, roses in ovals, micromosaic, tesserae are yellow, red, pale blue, and white, recently re-plated in gold, 7.25 in. long. Value $145

**Bracelet**, marked "Weiss", 1942 – 1950s, red glass prong-set in brass, 7.25 in. long. (Collection of Debbie White). Value $150

**Bracelet**, clear glass prong-set in brass, 1930s – 1940s, detachable guard chain, 7 in. long. (Collection of Debbie White). Value $75

Bracelet, 1940s – 1960s, marked "Siam" and "Sterling", bypass, Asian motif in red enamel, 2 in. diameter. (Courtesy of Lisa L. Olson). Value $150

Bracelets (2) 1932 – 1961, marked "S. Kirk & Son Sterling", repoussé pattern, each 2 in. diameter. (Courtesy of Lisa L. Olson). Value $450

**Bracelet**, Mid-Century Modern, marked "750", 1940s – 1950s, rose and yellow gold, 37.9 dwt. 7.75 in long. (Courtesy of Lisa L. Olson). Value $2,200

**Bracelet**, Mid-Century Modern, 1940s –1950s, hand made, brass and steel, 3 in. diameter. (Collection of Barbara Seaman). Value $35

**Bracelet**, Mid-Century Modern, 1940s –1950s, brass and steel, 3 in. diameter. (Collection of Barbara Seaman). Value $65

**Bracelet**, Asian, 1930s – 1940s, marked "made in Siam" and "Sterling", traditional figures, hand engraved, niello enameling, 6.25 in. long. (Courtesy of Cristina Romeo). Value $350

**Bracelet**, Mid-Century Modern, 1940s – 1950s, patterned link bracelet of hand-hammered aluminum, 7.25 in. long. (Courtesy of Joy Ste. Marie). Value $75

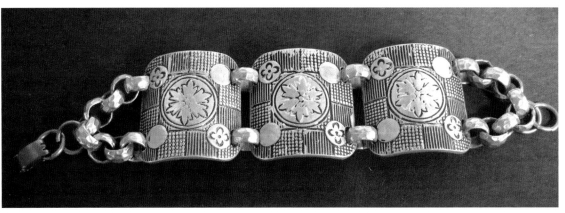

**Bracelet**, Mid-Century Modern, 1940s – 1950s, oak leaf and plaid pattern, link bracelet of hand-hammered aluminum, 7.25 in. long. (Courtesy of Joy Ste. Marie). Value $75

**Charm Bracelet**, 1950s – 1960s, marked "14k", link bracelet, cast charms, some moveable, 7.5 in. long. (Collection of Navon Vance). Value $950

**Bracelet**, 1950s - 1960s, amber colored and multi-tone glass, prong-set in brass, 8 in. long. (Collection of Debbie White). Value $160

**Bracelet**, 1930s – 1940s, white glass beads, expandable band, 2.75 in. diameter. (Collection of Debbie White). Value $45

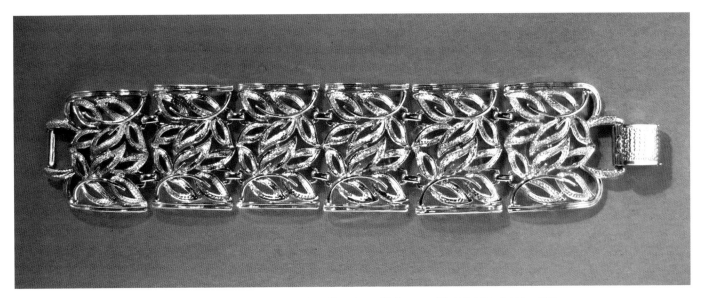

**Bracelet**, Corocraft, 1950 – 1960s, silver-toned stylized leaf motif, 7.25 in. long. (Collection of Debbie White). Value $85

**Bracelet**, Pop Art, Lea Stein, 1960s, celluloid spangle-pattern leaf motif, 2.15 in. diameter. (Courtesy of Roberta Knauer Mullings, G.G.). Value $150

**Bracelet**, Pop Art, Tortolani, 1960s, antiqued base metal with high relief of zodiac figures, 2 in. high, marked "©Tortolani". (Courtesy of Roberta Knauer Mullings, G.G.). Value $400

**Bracelet**, Victorian Revival, 1960s, buckle motif in 18 karat gold, 4.85 oz. 10.75 in. long. (Courtesy of Roberta Knauer Mullings, G.G.). Value $3,100

**Bracelet**, marked "Monet", 1950s – 1960s, stylize leaf motif, gold-tone plating with guard chain, 7.25 in long. (Collection of Debbie White). Value $85

# Brooches

**Brooch**, late Georgian, German, 1810 – 1830, feather motif of rose-cut spinel, garnet, natural pearl, gold, 1.938 in. long. (Author's Collection). Value $800

**Brooch**, late Georgian, 1810 – 1830, foil-backed topaz, seed pearls, mother-of-pearl mounting in silver, 0.813 in. wide. (Author's Collection). Value $400

**Brooch**, late Georgian, 1800 – 1825, mine-cut paste set in silver, 0.938 in. wide, replaced safety. (Author's Collection). Value $125

**Brooch**, late Georgian/early Victorian, 1825 – 1840, oval amethyst, approximately 7 carats, 18 karat gold mounting, 1.25 in. wide. (Courtesy of Ebert and Company). Value $1,400

**Brooch**, late Georgian/early Victorian, 1820 – 1840, woven hair under quartz crystal, rolled gold. (Chain safety later addition). Value $350

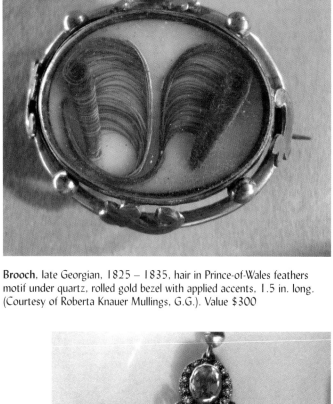

**Brooch**, late Georgian, 1825 – 1835, hair in Prince-of-Wales feathers motif under quartz, rolled gold bezel with applied accents, 1.5 in. long. (Courtesy of Roberta Knauer Mullings, G.G.). Value $300

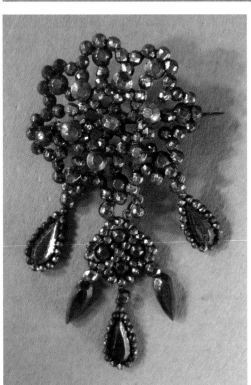

**Brooch**, late Georgian, 1825 – 1835, cut-steel riveted to brass mounts, girandole style. (Courtesy of Roberta Knauer Mullings, G.G.). Value $400

**Brooch/Pendant**, late Georgian, 1810 – 1830, Equilateral cross of gold, cannetille work, set with Topaz and natural pearls 2.5 in. long. (Courtesy of Roberta Knauer Mullings, G.G.). Value $2,400

Brooch, late Georgian, English date letter for Sheffield 1805, girandole style, cabochon turquoise, rose gold, 1.125 in. long. (Courtesy of Lisa L. Olson). Value $1,500

Brooch/Pendant, early Victorian, 1835 – 1845, shell cameo, ¾ portrait of a woman with a letter, rolled gold, 1.25 in. high. (Courtesy of finderskeepersvintage.com). Value $325

Brooch, early Victorian, 1837 – 1860, hard stone cameo portrait of a bacchante maiden, 18 karat gold mounting with grape leaves and scrolls. (Courtesy of Ebert and Company). Value $1,200

**Brooch**, early Victorian, 1837 – 1860, woven hair, 3 in. long. (Courtesy of Roberta Knauer Mullings, G.G.). $350

**Brooch**, early Victorian, late Classical style, 1840s, rolled gold with woven hair, 2.75 in. long. (Courtesy of Roberta Knauer Mullings, G.G.). Value $600

**Circle Pin**, early Victorian, Rococo Revival, rose-cut garnets set closed back in rolled gold, 1 in. diameter. (Courtesy of Roberta Knauer Mullings, G.G.). Value $295

Brooch, late Georgian/early Victorian, 1825 – 1850, hair and seed pearl under quartz, 18k, 2.25 in. long. (Courtesy of Diana Miller, Out of the Attic). Value $400

Brooch, early Victorian, 1845 – 1860, bog oak with hound, harp, and tower, 2.625 in. long. (Courtesy of Diana Miller, Out of the Attic). Value $225

Brooch, early Victorian, 1850s – 1860s, hand-painted portrait of a young girl holding a squirrel, porcelain, bezel is a buckle motif, 2.25 in. high. (Courtesy of Lisa L. Olson). Value $600

Brooch, early Victorian, 1840s – 1850s, deer in a forest, Vulcanite, 2.125 in. high. (Courtesy of Lisa L. Olson). Value $175

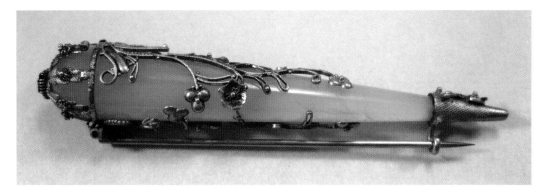

Brooch, early Victorian, 1837 – 1860, dirk of chalcedony, rolled gold with trefoils, 3 in. long. (Courtesy of Lisa L. Olson). Value $275

Brooch, early/mid Victorian, 1855 – 1865, portrait of Mary, hand painted on porcelain, rolled gold bezel, 3.5 in. high. (Courtesy of Cristina Romeo). Value $600

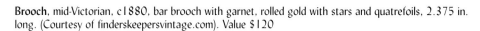

Brooch, mid-Victorian, c1880, bar brooch with garnet, rolled gold with stars and quatrefoils, 2.375 in. long. (Courtesy of finderskeepersvintage.com). Value $120

Brooch, mid-Victorian, c1880, tree branch with floral accents, rolled gold, 2.25 in. long. (Courtesy of finderskeepersvintage.com). Value $150

**Brooch**, mid-Victorian, 1860 – 1880, Scottish Agate with Celtic cross, silver, 1.938 in. diameter. (Author's Collection). Value $1,650

**Brooch**, mid-Victorian, Gothic Revival, 1860 – 1880s, Armagh Cathedral carved in bog oak, 2 in. diameter. Value $185

**Brooch**, mid-Victorian, 1860 – 1880, Etruscan Revival with granulation and a mine-cut diamond, approximately 0.50 carat, gold 2.5 in. long. (Courtesy of Ebert and Company). Value $600

**Brooch**, mid-Victorian, 1870s, natural foliage encased in amber, beaded silver bezel, 2.5 in. wide. Value $95

**Brooch**, mid-Victorian, 1860s – 1870s, a lady's hand carved in jet, 2 in. wide. Value $110

**Brooch**, mid-Victorian, 1860 – 1880, hard-stone cameo portrait of Hebe serving nectar, rolled gold bezel, 1.625 in. wide. (Courtesy of Roberta Knauer Mullings, G.G.). Value $600

**Brooch**, mid-Victorian, 1860 – 1880, lava or Meerschaum cameo, steel bezel, rolled gold frame, small chip on chin, 1.75 in. high. (Courtesy of Roberta Knauer Mullings, G.G.). Value $400

**Brooch**, mid-Victorian, 1860 –1880, lava cameo, double ¾ length portraits, 12 karat gold bezel, 2 in. high. (Courtesy of Roberta Knauer Mullings, G.G.). Value $350

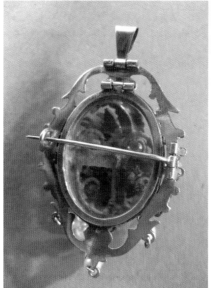

**Brooch/Pendant**, mid-Victorian, 1870 – 1880s, Persian turquoise, natural pearls and garnets, reverse with compartment for hair, 2.25 in. long. (Courtesy of Roberta Knauer Mullings, G.G.). Value $885

**Brooch**, mid-Victorian, 1860s – 1880s, plaited ribbon under quartz, gold-filled, shield-shaped bezel, 1.75 in. long. (Courtesy of Roberta Knauer Mullings, G.G.). Value $230

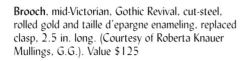

**Brooch**, mid-Victorian, Gothic Revival, cut-steel, rolled gold and taille d'epargne enameling, replaced clasp, 2.5 in. long. (Courtesy of Roberta Knauer Mullings, G.G.). Value $125

**Brooch**, mid-Victorian, Insect pin, garnet eyes, jasper body, gold-filled, 1.75 in. long. (Courtesy of Roberta Knauer Mullings, G.G.). Value $250

**Brooch**, mid-Victorian, c1880, woven hair bar pin, rolled gold 2.125 in. long. (Courtesy of Diana Miller, Out of the Attic). Value $100

**Brooch/Pendant**, mid-Victorian, c1865, hard stone cameo, natural pearl, rose gold, hand assembled, replaced safety, 2.25 in. long. (Courtesy of Diana Miller, Out of the Attic). Value $650

Brooch, mid-Victorian, 1870s, shield-shaped, rolled gold top, 1.5 in. wide. (Courtesy of Lisa L. Olson). Value $100

Brooch, mid-Victorian, 1870s, lover's knot with old European cut diamonds (0.27 total carats), rolled gold, 1.6 in long. (Collection of Barbara Seaman). Value $280

Brooch, mid-Victorian insect pin (bee), 1860s – 1870s, amber glass, gold-plated over copper, 1.375 in. long. (Collection of Debbie White). Value $150

Brooch/Pendant, mid-Victorian, marked "14K" 1860s – 1870s, shell cameo with neo-classical figures, 2" high. (Collection of Navon Vance). Value $600

Brooch, Arts & Crafts, landscape, c1900, hand-painted on porcelain, silver-plated, 3 in. wide. (Courtesy of finderskeepersvintage.com). Value $95

Brooch, late Victorian, 1880s, portrait of Dante in pietra dura, 1.375 in. diameter. (Author's Collection). Value $600

Brooch, Arts & Crafts, 1890s, fresh water pearl, rose gold, 1.75 in wide. (Courtesy of Ebert and Company). Value $350

Brooch, marked "800", 1890 – 1915, Arts & Crafts reverse-painted landscape (palm trees) with butterfly wings, 1.7 in. long. (Courtesy of Diana Miller, Out of the Attic). Value $75

Brooch, Arts & Crafts, 1900 – 1920, grapes and leaves of amber, 2.5 in. high. (Courtesy of Diana Miller, Out of the Attic). Value $175

Brooch, Arts and Crafts, c1900, marked "900", ivory rose, and silver leaf motif, 2.5 in. long. (Courtesy of Lisa L. Olson). $165

**Brooch**, Arts & Crafts, 1870s – 1880s, gold in quartz, rolled-gold bezel, 0.9 in. wide. (Collection of Navon Vance). **Value** $300

**Brooch**, Aesthetic Period, c1880, Swiss Souvenir, Edelweiss, horn, and bell of mother-of-pearl and silver, 1.5 in. wide. Value $55

**Brooch**, Aesthetic Period, c1890, Native American arrowhead, rolled-gold mounting, 1.3 in. long. Value $55

**Brooch**, late-Victorian, Aesthetic style, channel set garnets, rolled gold, 2.5 in. long. (Collection of Heather Gates). Value $165

Brooch, Arts & Crafts, marked
"14k", 1880 – 1915, wire work,
1.5 in. wide. (Collection of M.Q.
Iacovetti). Value $140

Brooch/Pendant, late Victorian, 1880s,
rose-cut garnets, gold-topped, replaced
safety, 2 in. high. (Collection of M.Q.
Iacovetti). Value $375

Brooch/Pendant, late Victorian, c1900,
porcelain with dark blue ground, reserves
with transfer printed portrait, gilt and
tinted accents, bezel set in rolled gold,
1.875 in. diameter. (Courtesy of Roberta
Knauer Mullings, G.G.). Value $150

**Brooch/Pendant**, German, Tyrolean boy, 1880s – c1900, 2.5 in. high, hand-painted portrait on porcelain, bezel-set, rolled gold frame. (Courtesy of Roberta Knauer Mullings, G.G.). Value $650

**Brooch**, late Victorian, 1880s – c1900, Scottish grouse foot, base metal and prong-set glass, 3.75 in. long. (Courtesy of Roberta Knauer Mullings, G.G.). Value $225

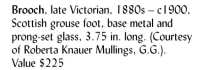

**Brooch**, late Victorian, 1895 – 1901, shell cameo portrait, marked "14K", 2.25 in. high. (Courtesy of Roberta Knauer Mullings, G.G.). Value $400

**Brooch/Pendant**, late Victorian, 1880s – c1900, shell cameo of three graces, marked "14K", 1.5 in high. (Courtesy of Roberta Knauer Mullings, G.G.). Value $275

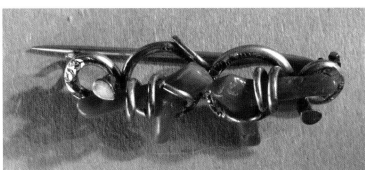

**Brooch**, late Victorian, rolled gold with branch coral, 1.75 in. long. (Courtesy of Roberta Knauer Mullings, G.G.). Value $95

**Brooch**, late Victorian, Neo-Classical Revival, sulfide muse, butterfly wings background, marked "England" and "Sterling Silver" 0.75 in. diameter. (Courtesy of Roberta Knauer Mullings, G.G.). Value $275

Posy Pin, late Victorian, 1881 – c1900, guilloché enamel, marked "Sterling" 2 in. long. (Courtesy of Roberta Knauer Mullings, G.G.). Value $125

Bar Pin, late Victorian, c1890, 10.07ct amethyst set in 14 karat gold, 3.2dwt. marked "14k", 2.25 in long. (Courtesy of Roberta Knauer Mullings, G.G.). Value $375

Brooch and Pendant, marked "Caldwell 9 22 91", small old European cut brilliant, vermeil and enameled "Daughters of the American Revolution", 1.75 in. high. (Courtesy of Roberta Knauer Mullings, G.G.). Value $1,800

**Brooch**, late Victorian, marked "Alpaca", flower of micromosaics, Arts & Crafts bezel, 1.125 in. long. (Courtesy of Diana Miller, Out of the Attic). Value $65

**Brooch**, late Victorian, thistles and foliage, amethyst glass, brass, 2.5 in. long. (Courtesy of Diana Miller, Out of the Attic). Value $125

**Brooch**, neo-Classical revival, 1880 – 1910, hand painted mother and child on porcelain, 1.5 in. diameter. (Courtesy of Diana Miller, Out of the Attic). Value $185

Brooch, 1880s, portrait fan of painted ivory, 3.375 in. long. (Courtesy of Lisa L. Olson). Value $150

Brooch, marked "depose", 1900 – 1920, insect of carved horn, 2.25 in. long. (Courtesy of Lisa L. Olson). Value $100

Brooch, 1880s – 1910, crescent moon and star motif with garnets, rolled gold, replaced safety, 1.375 in. long. (Courtesy of Lisa L. Olson). Value $275

**Brooch**, late Victorian, marked "800", 1885 – 1895, Egyptian Revival motif, scarab in vermeil, ceramic body, red, blue, green, and amber champlevé enamel, 1.125 in. long. (Courtesy of Lisa L. Olson). Value $175

**Brooch**, late Victorian, 1880s, micromosaic of a dove and flowers, turquoise, white, pink and green tesserae, pelleted accents, 1 in. long. (Courtesy of Lisa L. Olson). **Value $165**

**Brooch**, late Victorian, 1880s, archeological revival, micromosaic of an insect, white, red, and green tesserae, 1 in. long. (Courtesy of Lisa L. Olson). **Value $590**

**Brooch**, late Victorian, 1880s – 1890s, spider in a web of cast brass, 1 in. diameter. (Courtesy of Cristina Romeo). Value $65

**Brooch**, late Victorian, 1880s, cameo portrait of a man and a woman, hand-painted on porcelain, cast bronze setting, 2.25 in. diameter. (Collection of Navon Vance). Value $125

**Brooch**, late Victorian, Edwardian, 1890s – 1910, gold rush mining motif, marked "800", 2 in. long. (Collection of Debbie White). Value $300

**Brooch**, Art Nouveau, c1900, dragonfly of brass and glass, 4.375 in. wide. Value $100

**Brooch**, Art Nouveau, Sheffield hallmarks for 1914, sterling with cloisonné and basse-taille enamel, floral motif, 2 in. long. (Courtesy of Roberta Knauer Mullings, G.G.). Value $195

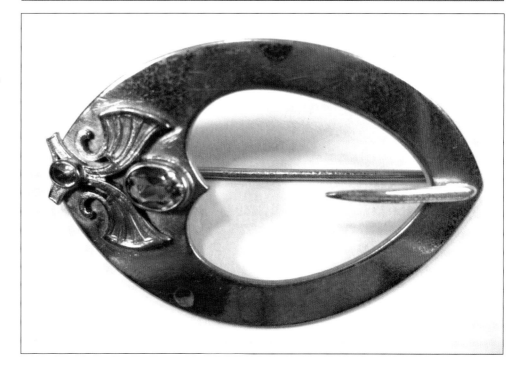

**Sash pin**, Art Nouveau, 1885 – 1910, rolled gold and bezel-set glass stones. (Courtesy of Roberta Knauer Mullings, G.G.). Value $75

**Photo Brooch**, Art Nouveau, 1890 – 1920, stylized peacock frame of cast bronze, 1.75 in. long. (Courtesy of Diana Miller, Out of the Attic). Value $95

**Brooch**, 1915 – 1920, dragonfly of navy Bakelite, 3.75 in. long. (Courtesy of Lisa L. Olson). Value $275

**Brooch**, marked "10k", 1895 – 1915, four-leaf clover in basse-taille enamel, fresh water pearl, 1.0625 in. long. (Courtesy of Lisa L. Olson). Value $250

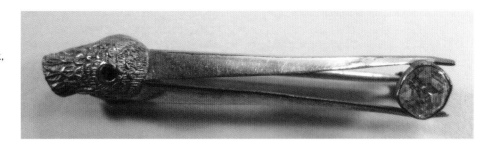

Brooch, Art Nouveau, 1885 – 1910, stork holding a mine-cut paste in his beak, rolled gold, 2.25 in. long. (Courtesy of Lisa L. Olson). Value $95

Brooch, Art Nouveau, 1890s – 1920, marked "Sterling", female portrait with pansies, replaced safety, 2.875 in. long. (Courtesy of Lisa L. Olson). Value $300

Brooch, Art Nouveau, 1895 – 1915, floral motif with fresh water pearl, guilloché enamel, 14k gold, 1.125 in. high. (Collection of Debbie White). Value $250

Brooch, Art Nouveau (1885 – 1925), floral motif, marked "Sterling", 3 in. long. (Courtesy of Roberta Knauer Mullings, G.G.). Value $225

**Brooch**, Belle Epoque, 1915 – 1925 opaque glass cameo, brass mounting, 2 in. high. (Courtesy of Roberta Knauer Mullings, G.G.). Value $50

**Brooch/Pendant**, Belle Époque, marked "14K", 1920 – 1925, shell cameo portrait, diamond accent, white gold, 2.5 in. high. (Courtesy of Diana Miller, Out of the Attic). Value $325

**Brooch**, late Victorian/Edwardian, Daughters of the Nile motif, marked "14k" white gold top, yellow gold base, ivory and diamond, 2.5 in. long. (Courtesy of Cristina Romeo) Value $375

**Brooch**, Gothic Revival Style, c1920, marked "Italy" and "800", hand-painted portrait, porcelain, vermeil setting, 1.3 in. high. (Courtesy of finderskeepersvintage. com). Value $125

**Brooch**, late Victorian, 1880 – c1900, star motif, micromosaic, replaced safety, 1.125 in diameter. (Courtesy of finderskeepersvintage.com). Value $45

**Brooch**, Edwardian, c1910 Union case, bacchante portrait, 2.25 in. diameter. (Courtesy of Roberta Knauer Mullings, G.G.). Value $75

**Brooch**, Edwardian/Belle Époque, 1900 – 1915, marked "14k", diamonds (0.24cts total weight) white gold mounting, 2.875 in. long. Value $300

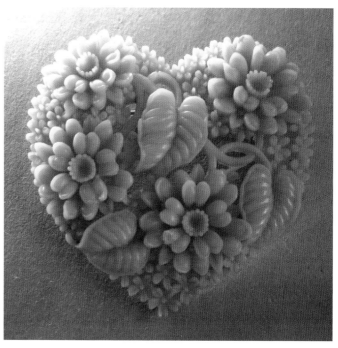

**Brooch/Pendant**, Belle Époque, 1890 – 1920, shell cameo, white gold, marked "14K", 2.25 in high. (Courtesy of Roberta Knauer Mullings, G.G.). Value $275

**Brooch**, Belle Époque, 1920s - 1930s, celluloid, heart-shaped, floral motif, 2.5 in high. (Courtesy of Roberta Knauer Mullings, G.G.). Value $50

**Brooch**, Belle Époque, 1920s – 1930s, floral motif, pietra dura bezel-set, marked "Sterling", 1.75 in. long. (Courtesy of Roberta Knauer Mullings, G.G.). Value $225

Brooch, Colonial Revival, 1920s, reverse painted glass, butterfly wings background, marked "made in England" and "Sterling", 1.5 in. long. (Courtesy of Roberta Knauer Mullings, G.G.). Value $135

Brooch, Edwardian, sulfide blue bells, butterfly wings background, marked "made in England" and "Sterling" 1.625 in. high. (Courtesy of Roberta Knauer Mullings, G.G.). Value $250

Brooch, Scottish agate, 1920s, silver-toned base metal, 1.4 in. diameter. (Courtesy of Roberta Knauer Mullings, G.G.). Value $250

Brooch, Belle Époque, 1890 – 1915, flower and leaves, hand-painted on porcelain, 1.5 in. wide. (Courtesy of Diana Miller, Out of the Attic). Value $65

**Brooch**, marked "925", 1925 – 1940, feather pin with basse-taille enamel in light blue, brown, black, and beige, 2.875 in. long. (Courtesy of Lisa L. Olson). $175

**Brooch**, 1890 – 1915, lava cameo of Diana, gold-plated, 1.25 in. high. (Courtesy of Lisa L. Olson). Value $140

**Brooch**, marked "800", 1890 – 1915, bird on a branch of vermeil, 1.0625 in. long. (Courtesy of Lisa L. Olson). Value $75

**Brooch**, 1910 – 1920, circle pin with cultured pearl, gold, 1.25 in. long. (Courtesy of Lisa L. Olson). Value $150

Brooch, Art Deco, 1917 – 1925, floral motif, crystal in white base metal, 3.5 in. high. (Courtesy of finderskeepersvintage.com). Value $110

Brooch, Belle Époque, 1890 – 1915 shell cameo, brass embossed bezel, brass tassel, replaced safety and pin stem, overall height 2.6 in. (Courtesy of Roberta Knauer Mullings, G.G.). Value $65

Brooch, Asian Art Deco, floral motif of cinnabar, brass-plated, 2.75 in. long. (Courtesy of finderskeepersvintage.com). Value $85

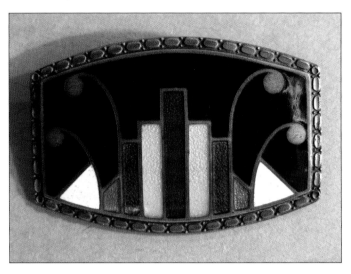

**Brooch**, Art Deco, 1917 – 1925, champlevé enameling on white base metal, 2.25 in. long. (Courtesy of Roberta Knauer Mullings, G.G.). Value $45

**Converted Brooch**, modern Berlin iron, dated 1916, double-sided medal, front has kneeling woman and the phrase "In Eiserner Zeit" ("In Iron Time"), verso phrase is "Gold gab ich zur wehr eisen nahm ich zur ehr" ("Gold I gave to the resistance, iron took I to honour") Value $125

**Brooch**, Art Deco, 1920s, onyx, marcasite, and sterling, marked "Sterling", 1.75 in. long. (Courtesy of Roberta Knauer Mullings, G.G.). Value $100

Brooch, Art Deco, heart and key in red
Bakelite, 5 in. high. Brooch was featured on
the cover of *Life Magazine*, April 28, 1941.
(Courtesy of Diana Miller, Out of the Attic).
Value $1,525

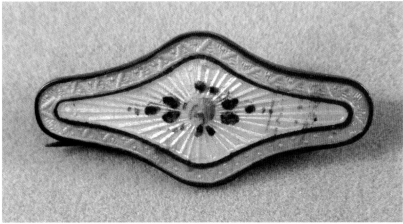

Brooch, Belle Époque, marked "made in
Czechoslovakia", 1918 – 1925, basse-
taille enamel with hand painted rose on
copper, 1.5 in. long. (Courtesy of Diana
Miller, Out of the Attic). Value $70

Brooch, Art Deco, 1936 – 1940s, gold,
black and gray enamel, paste accents,
encased in Lucite, 2.25 in. long. (Courtesy
of Diana Miller, Out of the Attic). Value
$45

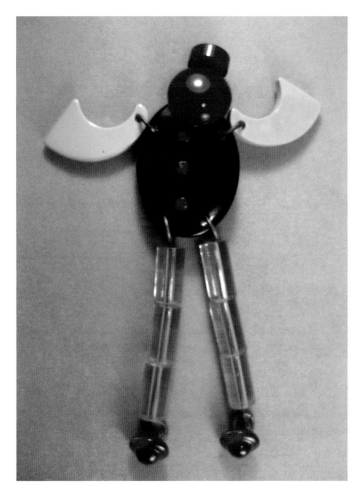

Brooch, Art Deco, 1917 – 1939, bellhop in red, yellow, and black Bakelite and lucite 5 in. long. (Courtesy of Diana Miller, Out of the Attic). Value $600

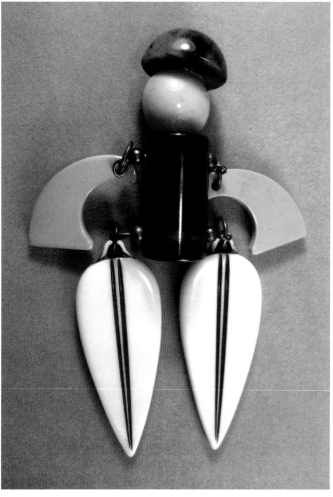

Brooch, Art Deco, 1917 – 1939, figure in butterscotch, tortoise, and beige Bakelite and lucite 5 in. long. (Courtesy of Diana Miller, Out of the Attic). Value $600

Brooch, 1930s – 1940s, Scotty dog sulfide in Lucite, painted wood backing, 2 in. long. (Courtesy of Lisa L. Olson). Value $75

**Scatter Pins**, marked "Coro", 1917 – 1935, cat and bird, black and yellow enamel, cut glass, silver base metal, overall length of 2.78 in. (Courtesy of Lisa L. Olson). Value $50

**Brooch**, Art Deco, 1917 – 1930s, Bakelite cherries, 4.75 in. high. (Courtesy of Lisa L. Olson). Value $350

**Brooch**, Art Deco, 1917 – 1930s, borzoi hounds, beige and black tinted celluloid, 2.875 in. long. (Courtesy of Lisa L. Olson). Value $50

**Brooch**, Art Deco, 1930s –1940s, Scotty Dog in Bakelite, glass eyes painted bow, nose and tongue. (Collection of Barbara Seaman). Value $85

**Brooch**, pansy pin, 1925 – 1935, marcasite and hand-painted enamel, 3 in. long. (Collection of Debbie White). Value $65

**Brooch**, Bakelite, carved horse head with metal reins, 1930s, 2.5 in. high. (Collection of Debbie White). Value $345

**Brooch**, Art Deco, 1930s – 1940s, paddle boat set with multi-colored glass, cast base metal (wheel turns) 1.25 in. long. (Collection of Debbie White). Value $75

Brooch, Patriotic motif, 1939 – 1950, enameled base metal, 3 in long. (Courtesy of Roberta Knauer Mullings, G.G.). Value $75

Brooch and Locket, Sweetheart brooch with attached separate locket mounted hand-painted mother-of-pearl, gold toned, brooch is 2 in. wide, locket is 2.75 in. high. (Courtesy of Roberta Knauer Mullings, G.G.). Value $75

Brooch, marked "Cini" & "Sterling", 1945 – 1950s, insect motif, blue glass, 1 in. long. (Courtesy of Diana Miller, Out of the Attic). Value $100

**Brooch**, marked "Sterling", 1941 – 1950, "V" for victory, red, white, and blue glass, 0.875 in. long. (Courtesy of Diana Miller, Out of the Attic). Value $125

**Brooch**, Mid-Century Modern, marked "Regency", 1940s, uranium-based Vaseline glass and rhinestones, shown at left under black light, prong set, 2.375 in. diameter. (Courtesy of Diana Miller, Out of the Attic). Value $95

**Brooch**, 1940s – 1950s, attributed to Takahashi, pheasant of dyed and painted ivory, 4.5 in. long. (Courtesy of Lisa L. Olson). Value $200

Brooch, 1950s, marked "18k",
floral motif, rubies, diamonds,
Florentine finish, 3.5 in. long.
(Courtesy of Lisa L. Olson). Value
$650

Brooch, marked "18k", 1940s – 1950s,
butterfly set with 40 diamonds, white,
yellow, and rose gold, 2.25 in high.
(Courtesy of Lisa L. Olson). Value
$1,500

Brooch, marked "Siam" and "Sterling",
1940s, yellow champlevé enamel, 1.75
in. high. (Courtesy of Cristina Romeo)
Value $75

**Brooch**, butterfly motif, 1940s – 1950s, glass prong-set in die-stamped brass, 3 in long. (Collection of Debbie White). Value $55

**Brooch**, marked "Weiss", 1942 – 1950s. pansy with prong-set, smoke colored glass, silver-toned base metal, 2 in. diameter. (Collection of Debbie White). Value $160

**Brooch**, marked "Weiss", 1942 – 1950s, pansy with pavé-set blue glass, enamel with hand-painted accents, gold-washed, faux pearl center, 1.5 in. high. (Collection of Debbie White). Value $195

**Brooch**, Art Deco, 1930s – 1940s, guitar of multi-colored glass stones, prong and bezel-set, pewter-toned base metal, 4 in. long. (Collection of Debbie White). Value $85

Brooch, marked "Hattie Carnegie" 1950s-1960s, abstract floral with black and white glass, pewter-toned metal, 2 in. diameter. (Collection of Debbie White). Value $85

Brooch, 1950s, marked "14k", bow motif, rose and yellow gold, 2.25 in. wide. (Courtesy of finderskeepersvintage.com). Value $275

Brooch, marked "Art", 1940s, Renaissance Revival style, shield shapes set with glass, faux turquoise, gold-toned, 3.5 in. high. (Collection of Debbie White). Value $75

Brooch, Mid-Century Modern, 1940s – 1950s, marked "Coro" and "Sterling", stylized floral and bow motif set with pastes, 3.875 in. long. (Courtesy of finderskeepersvintage.com). Value $100

**Brooch/Pendant**, Victorian Revival, 1950s – 1960s, smoked glass prong set in gold-toned base metal, leaf accents, 2 in. high. (Courtesy of Roberta Knauer Mullings, G.G.). Value $85

**Brooch**, Moderne, c1940, leaf motif set with crystals, gold-toned, 2.5 in. long, marked "McClelland Barclay". (Courtesy of Roberta Knauer Mullings, G.G.). Value $165

**Brooch**, Mid-Century Modern, 1958+, Russian, rhodochrosite, silver, 2.125 in. long. (Courtesy of Diana Miller, Out of the Attic). Value $285

Brooch, marked "Ming's Ivory",
1950s – 1960s, leaf motif, dyed
ivory, 3.5 in. long. (Courtesy of Lisa
L. Olson). Value $185

Brooch, 1950s – 1960s,
marked "Boucher", rose set
with pastes, Florentine finish,
3.25 in. long. (Collection of
Barbara Seaman). Value $95

Brooch, 1950s – 1960s, marked
"14k", tree branch and leaves with
6 – 6.5mm cultured pearls, 2.375
in. high. (Collection of Navon
Vance). Value $475

**Brooch**, 1950s – 1960s, coralene glass cameo, floral print, gold-plated, 2 in. high. (Collection of Navon Vance). Value $75

**Brooch**, Alice Caviness, enamel over Sterling, two parrots on a branch, 1.5 in. high. (Collection of Debbie White). Value $120

**Brooch**, marked "Czecho", butterfly motif, prong-set glass, enamel, brass, 1.75 in. wide. (Collection of Debbie White). Value $65

**Brooch**, marked "Nettie Rosenstein", 1950s, three parrots on a branch, enamel over Sterling, glass and marcasite, 1.75 in. wide. (Collection of Debbie White). Value $150

**Brooch**, marked "David Andersen", 1940s – 1950s, Sterling pansy, yellow orange and green enameling, 1.5 in. wide. (Collection of Debbie White). Value $185

**Scatter Pins** (2) marked "Emmons", 1950s – 1960s, salamanders with red, prong-set pastes, pewter-toned metal, each 2.625 in. long. (Collection of Debbie White). Value $160

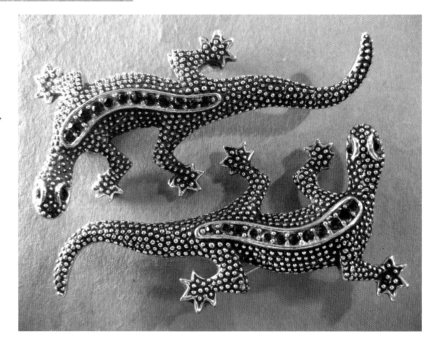

**Brooch**, marked "Art", 1950s – 1960s, faux turquoise, faux pearl, pastes, gold-tone plated, Florentine finish, flower and butterfly *en tremblant*, 2.5 in. high. (Collection of Debbie White). Value $175

**Brooch**, marked "Miriam Haskell", bow and bells, high polish and Florentine finish, gold-tone metal, 3 in. high. (Collection of Debbie White). Value $125

**Brooch**, marked "David Andersen", 1950s – 1960s, owl with guilloché enamel on sterling silver, 1.625 in. high. (Collection of Debbie White). Value $325

**Brooch**, marked "J. J.", 1950s – 1960s, rose set with marcasites, matte gold-tone finish, 2.25 in. long. (Collection of Debbie White). Value $165

Brooch, marked "Lang", 1945–1955, flower basket and butterfly in sterling, 3 in. long. (Collection of Debbie White). Value $225

Brooch, Mid-Century Modern, 1950s – 1960s, orange, white, and black glass; gold-tone plating, 2.5 in. long. (Collection of Debbie White). Value $150

Brooch, Pop Art, Lea Stein, 1960s, stripped celluloid fox, finding stamped "Lea Stein", "Paris". (Courtesy of Roberta Knauer Mullings, G.G.). Value $195

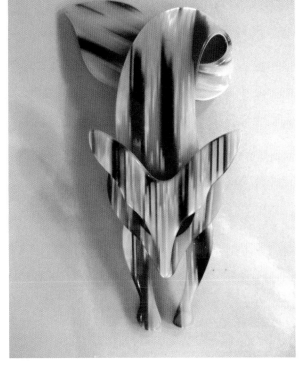

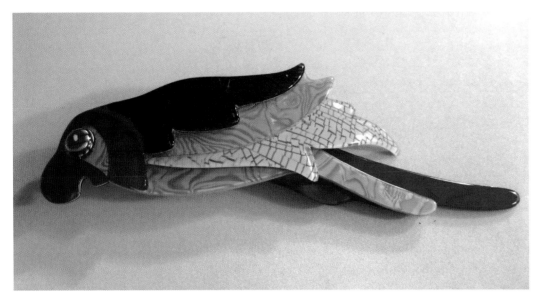

Brooch, Pop Art, Lea Stein, 1960s, multi-pattern celluloid parrot, 4.5 in. long, finding stamped "Lea Stein", "Paris". (Courtesy of Roberta Knauer Mullings, G.G.). $195

Brooches (2) Pop Art, 1960s, gold-wash over silver, enameled legs, glass eyes, marked "silver", each 2 in. high. (Courtesy of Roberta Knauer Mullings, G.G.). Value $325

Brooch, Pop Art, 1960s, Lea Stein, Christmas tree in black and white patterned celluloid, 3.625 in. long. (Courtesy of Roberta Knauer Mullings, G.G.). Value $195

Brooch, marked "Flair Craft 18k", 1960s, bee with pavé-set diamond wings, 1 in. long. (Courtesy of Lisa L. Olson). Value $325

# Chatelaines and Lorgnettes

**Watch Chatelaine**, early Victorian, 1840 – 1860, linked plates with attributes of music, original signet fob, gold-plated, 5.25 in. long. (Collection of M.Q. Iacovetti). Value $500

**Lorgnette**, late Victorian/Edwardian, marked "Sterling" and "Chadco", 1880s – c 1910, closed length is 3 in. (Collection of M.Q. Iacovetti). Value $285

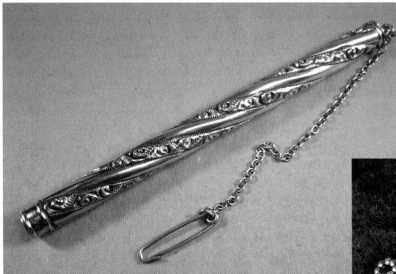

**Thermometer Chatelaine**, late Victorian, 1880s, marked "Sterling", embossed banded rose pattern, safety-pin clasp, 4.75 in. long. (Collection of M.Q. Iacovetti). Value $275

**Sewing Chatelaine**, late Victorian, cut-steel, 1880s, includes lorgnette, thimble and thimble case, whistle, tape measure, button hook, and tooth pick, hook plate is 3.5 in. long. (Collection of M.Q. Iacovetti). Value $1,000

**Chatelaine**, late Victorian, hook plate with English Hallmarks for 1894, includes thimble bucket, needle or bodkin case, later stamp case, hook plate is 2.5 in. long. (Collection of M.Q. Iacovetti). Value $1,200

**Lorgnette**, late Victorian/Edwardian, tortoise, 1880s – c 1910, closed length is 3.75 in. (Collection of M.Q. Iacovetti). Value $185

**Dance Chatelaine**, late Victorian, 1880s, slide chain, note pad and mechanical pencil, slide chain is 54 in. long, note pad is 3 in. (Collection of M.Q. Iacovetti). Value $350

**Pince-nez Chatelaine**, heart-shaped pin, gold-filled, base metal chain and hook, 3 in. long. (Courtesy of Roberta Knauer Mullings, G.G.). Value $60

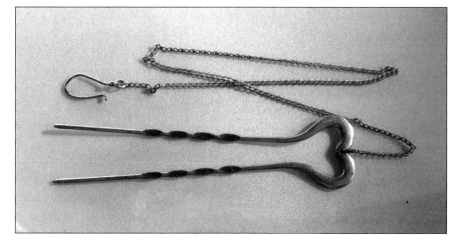

**Eye Glass Chatelaine**, marked "Ketchum and McDougal", retractable chain, silver-plated, 1 in. diameter. (Courtesy of Diana Miller, Out of the Attic). Value $65

**Chatelaine**, late Victorian, sterling, Birmingham hallmark for 1900, original attachments (thimble replaced), overall length of 14". (Courtesy of Roberta Knauer Mullings, G.G.). Value $1,400

# Combs

**Hairpin**, Belle Époque, 1910 – 1920s, celluloid with pastes, 3.125 in. long. (Author's Collection). Value $45

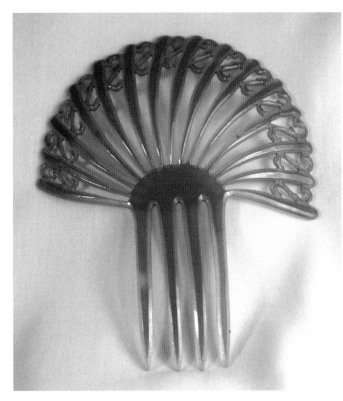

**Comb**, mid-Victorian, 1860 –1880, cyma curves of natural horn, 5 in. wide. (Author's Collection). Value $300

**Combs** (2), 1945- 1955, marked "Miriam Haskell", paste and faux pearl, gold-toned base metal, plastic combs, each is 2.625 in. wide. (Courtesy of finderskeepersvintage.com). Value $145

**Comb**, Aesthetic Period, 1870s – 1880s, cranes and chrysanthemums of dyed horn, 4.5 in. wide. (Courtesy of Ebert and Company). Value $565

# Dress Clips, Fur Clips, Lingerie Clips, and Money Clips

**Money Clip**, late Victorian, 1881 – c1900, watch cock cover set with cabochon paste, gold filled, 2.4 in. long. (Courtesy of Roberta Knauer Mullings, G.G.).Value $125

**Fur Clip**, Art Deco, 1917 – 1930s, acorns and leaves, red Bakelite, red celluloid, 2.875 in. long. (Author's Collection). Value $65

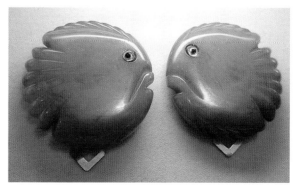

**Fur Clip**, Art Deco, 1930s, marked "Eisenberg Original", pastes in white metal, 3.75 in. high. (Courtesy of finderskeepersvintage.com). Value $165

**Dress Clips** (2), Art Deco, 1917 – 1930s, fish of Bakelite, glass eyes, each is 1.5 in. diameter. (Author's Collection). Value $250

**Duet**, Art Deco, 1920s – 1930s, convertible dress clip with geometric shapes and swirls set with approximately 4.84 carats of diamonds, platinum setting, 2.25 in. long . (Courtesy of Ebert and Company). Value $3,200

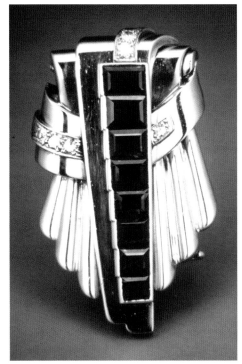

**Fur Clip**, Art Deco, 1920s – 1930s, calibré cut sapphires, diamond accents, champlevé enameling, platinum and white gold, 1.50 in. long. (Courtesy of Ebert and Company). Value $1,800

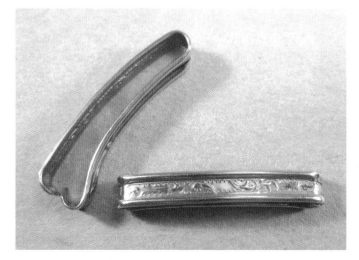

**Lingerie Clips**, Belle Époque, 1900 – 1925, marked "10k", embossed foliage, each clip is 0.875 in. long. (Collection of M.Q. Iacovetti). Value $85

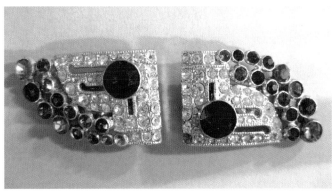

**Dress Clips**, Art Deco, patent date for 1933, white and colored glass, channel and glue set in cast base metal, each 2 in. long. (Courtesy of Roberta Knauer Mullings, G.G.). Value $150

**Fur Clip**, 1940s – 1950s, pansy set with amber and clear glass, enameled with hand-painted accents, silver-tone 1.75 in. long. (Collection of Debbie White). Value $275

# Earrings

Earrings, late Georgian, 1810 – 1830, coral and gold, removable pendants, 1.75 in. long. (Courtesy of Roberta Knauer Mullings, G.G.). Value $900

Earrings, late Georgian, 1800 – 1820, floral motif with fresh water pearls, rose gold, earrings are each 1.375 in. long. (Courtesy of Lisa L. Olson). Value $1,000

Earrings, late Georgian, 1800 – 1815, girandole style with mine-cut diamonds, cut-down collet in silver, each earring is 1.5 in. long. (Courtesy of Lisa L. Olson). Value $1,500

Earrings, early Victorian, 1840 – 1860, bog oak accented with shamrocks and twisted gold wire, Shepherd's hook fittings, 2.5 in. long. (Courtesy of Roberta Knauer Mullings, G.G.). Value $325

**Earrings**, early Victorian, 1850 – 1860, garnet and 14k gold, closed back settings, 2 in. long. (Courtesy of Roberta Knauer Mullings, G.G.). Value $450

**Earrings**, rolled gold with woven hair, kidney wires, 0.625 in. diameter. (Courtesy of Roberta Knauer Mullings, G.G.). Value $275

**Earrings**, mid-Victorian, 1870s, black glass, seed pearl, rolled gold, 3 in. long. (Author's Collection). Value $435

**Earrings**, mid-Victorian, 1870s, marked "750", filigree with tassels and pelleted accents, 2.5 in. long. (Author's Collection). Value $275

**Earrings**, mid-Victorian, 1870s, assembled and hinged jet, horseshoe shaped with engraved leaves, 2.5 in. high. (Courtesy of Roberta Knauer Mullings, G.G.). Value $400

**Earrings**, mid-Victorian, 1860 – 1880, pendant style, angel skin coral cameos with neoclassical motifs, gold filled, 3 in. long. (Courtesy of Roberta Knauer Mullings, G.G.). Value $425

**Earrings**, late Victorian, 1860 – 1880, pendant style, shell cameos with neoclassical motifs, rolled gold, 2.75 in. long. (Courtesy of Roberta Knauer Mullings, G.G.). Value $275

**Earrings**, late Victorian, 1837 – 1860, old European cut diamonds, approximately 1.50 cwt (total carat weight) gold mounting. (Courtesy of Ebert and Company). Value $3,500

**Earrings**, Arts & Crafts, 1880s, marked "925", rectangular cut lapis lazuli, sterling with pelleted accents, 1.375 in. high. (Author's Collection). Value $260

**Earrings**, late Victorian, Rococo Revival, hoop earrings with gadrooned leaves, gold, each earring is 1.5 in. high. (Collection of Heather Gates). Value $300

**Earrings**, mid/late Victorian, 1870s – 1880s, cut-steel riveted to brass mounts, post fittings, 2 in. long. (Courtesy of Roberta Knauer Mullings, G.G.). Value $250

**Earrings**, late Victorian, 1880s, rolled gold, channel-set garnets, taille d'epargne enameling, triangular posts with three drops; each earring is 1.75 in. long. (Collection of Heather Gates). Value $200

Earrings, late Victorian, 1881 – 1901, watch cock covers with cabochon pastes, rolled gold, pendant accents, each 0.875 in. diameter. (Courtesy of Roberta Knauer Mullings, G.G.). Value $350

Earrings, late Victorian, marked "Sterling", 1881 – c1900, clovers of vermeil and marcasite, Limoges enameled roses, each earring is 1.25 in. high. (Courtesy of Diana Miller, Out of the Attic). Value $95

Earrings, Art Nouveau, half-mourning, fresh water pearl and glass, lily motif, 1.25 in. long. (Courtesy of Roberta Knauer Mullings, G.G.). Value $165

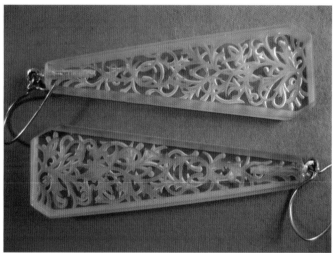

Earrings, Belle Époque, 1915 – 1925, triangular shaped crystal both sides etched with a vine motif, each 2.75 in. long. (Courtesy of Roberta Knauer Mullings, G.G.).Value $275

Earrings, Art Deco, 1930 – 1940, marked "Sterling", rectangular cut mother of pearl, beaded bezel, 0.625 in. high. (Author's Collection). Value $85

Earrings, early Art Deco, 1917 – 1925, crystal etched with a starburst, center paste, mounted in brass, each 2 in. long. (Courtesy of Roberta Knauer Mullings, G.G.). Value $65

Earrings, Art Deco, 1935 – 1945, orange branch coral, each earring is 1 in. diameter. (Courtesy of Diana Miller, Out of the Attic). Value $55

Earrings, Art Deco, marked "Sterling" 1920s – 1930s, smoky quartz, each approximately 18.6cts. (Courtesy of Lisa L. Olson). Value $500

Earrings, Art Deco, 1917 – 1925, marked "Germany" and "Sterling", faceted glass, Sterling, marcasites, each earring is 2.5 in. long. (Courtesy of Cristina Romeo). Value $150

Earrings, 1940s – 1950s, Victorian style, leaf motif, tourmaline, diamonds, gold, each earring is 1 in. high. (Collection of Navon Vance). Value $265

Earrings, marked "Nettie Rosenstein", 1950s –1960s, pavé-set paste in gold-toned metal, clip backs each 1 in. long. (Collection of Debbie White). Value $70

Earrings, marked "Trifari", Mid-Century Modern, 1940s – 1950s, button-shaped, white, gold stone glass, 0.875 in. diameter. (Collection of Debbie White). Value $60

Earrings, marked "Ciner", 1950s – 1960s, pavé-set paste in gold-toned metal, leaf accents, each 1 in. long. (Collection of Debbie White). Value $85

Earrings, marked "Nettie Rosenstein", 1950s – 1960s pavé-set, amber and clear paste in gold-toned metal, berry motif, each 1 in. long. (Collection of Debbie White). Value $85

Earrings, marked "Franco's" 1960s, cultured pearl, carnelian, quartz, gold-tone plating, ocean flora motif, each 1.125 in. high. (Collection of Debbie White). Value $55

Earrings, Pop Art, 1960s, marked "Razza" chicks in shell, chicks are carved bone, shell is plastic, earrings are each 0.625 in. high. (Collection of Navon Vance). Value $40

# Hat Pins

**Hatpin**, Edwardian, Sterling, London hallmarks for 1909, posé d'argent of an owl in flight set in tortoise, 1.5 in. wide, 10 in. stem, (Jodi Lenocker Collection). Value $330

**Hatpin**, Edwardian, attributed to Carrington & Company, marked "14 k", champlevé enameled leaves with freshwater pearls, 1 in. long, 7.5 in. stem (Jodi Lenocker Collection). Value $1,800

**Hatpin**, Edwardian, silver, clouté d'or, tortoise inlaid with silver pattern, 1.375 in. diameter, 10.5 in. stem (Jodi Lenocker Collection). Value $265

**Hatpin**, Edwardian, pierced and carved bone, 1.25 in. long, 9 in. stem (Jodi Lenocker Collection). Value $195

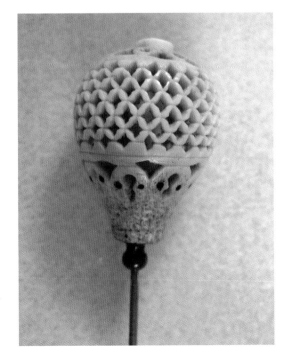

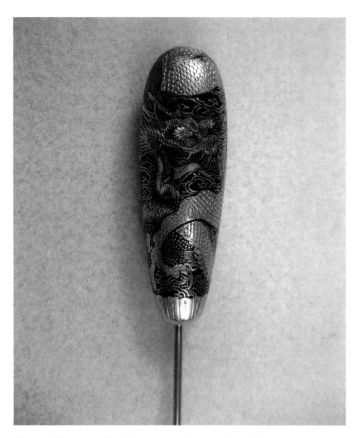

Hatpin, Edwardian, black-lacquered surface with hand-hammered Asian motifs in gold, 2 in. long, 10 in. stem (Jodi Lenocker Collection). Value $650

Hatpin, Late Victorian, 16 karat gold with granulation, cut amethyst, seed pearl accents, 0.75 in. long, 8 in. stem (Jodi Lenocker Collection). Value $400

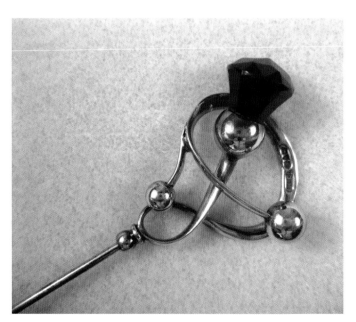

Hatpin, Edwardian, Sterling, Hallmarks for 1910, Charles Horner, glass thistle, 1.25 in. long, 10 in. stem (Jodi Lenocker Collection). Value $200

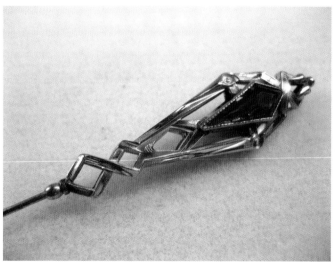

Hatpin, Arts and Crafts, amber glass lozenge, geometric setting, 2.5 in. long, 10.5 in. stem, (Jodi Lenocker Collection). Value $350

Hatpin/Compact, Edwardian, gold plated over brass, floral motif with orchids holds mirrored compact with original puff, 1.5 in. long, 12 in. stem (Jodi Lenocker Collection). Value $2,500

**Hatpin**, Late Victorian, micromosaic, floral motif, gold setting, 1.5 in. diameter, 7.75 in. stem (Jodi Lenocker Collection). Value $700

**Hatpin**, Edwardian, basse-taille enamel, hand painted floral accents, rolled gold, 1.5 in. diameter, 10 in. stem (Jodi Lenocker Collection). Value $450

**Hatpin**, Late Victorian/Edwardian, porcelain ball, transfer printed portrait, hand enhanced, silvered border, 1.25 in. diameter, 9 in. stem (Jodi Lenocker Collection). Value $550

**Hatpin**, Belle Époque, converted World War I military button, 1 in. diameter, 8 in stem (Jodi Lenocker Collection). Value $85

**Hatpin**, Late Victorian/Edwardian, triangle shape with basse-taille border, pastes, and green glass center, 1.5 in. long, 9 in. stem (Jodi Lenocker Collection). Value $475

**Hatpin**, Edwardian, Satsuma finish, geisha girl and small child, hand painted, 1.75 in. long, 9 in. stem (Jodi Lenocker Collection). Value $500

**Hatpin/Brooch**, Belle Époque, porcelain, transfer printed portrait, converts to a brooch, 1.5 in. long, 8 in. stem (Jodi Lenocker Collection). Value $450

**Hatpin/Vinaigrette**, Belle Époque, marked "14k" rectangular, tapered body, top opens to reveal scented cotton, 0.75 in. long, 8 in. stem (Jodi Lenocker Collection). Value $1,200

**Hatpin/Compass**, Belle Époque, 16 karat gold ball opens to reveal a compass, 0.75 in. diameter, 7 in. stem (Jodi Lenocker Collection). Value $475

**Hatpin**, Arts and Crafts, amber glass with snake motif, hand-hammered look, 1.75 in diameter, 10 in. stem (Jodi Lenocker Collection). Value $150

**Hatpin**, Art Nouveau, black carnival glass, stylized butterfly, 1.75 in. long, 9.5 in. stem (Jodi Lenocker Collection). Value $75

**Hatpin**, Art Nouveau, marked Link & Angell, marked "Sterling", Indian Chief Face and headdress executed in an Art Nouveau motif, 10.25 in. stem (Jodi Lenocker Collection). Value $375

**Jabot**, Art Deco, 1917 – 1930s, Celluloid and pastes, 3.125 in. long. (Author's Collection). Value $50

**Hatpin *en tremblant***, Belle Époque, bird in flight, glass accents, gilt base metal, 1.9375 in wide, 6.25 in. stem (Jodi Lenocker Collection). Value $200

# Lockets and Pendants

**Pendant**, late Georgan, 1820s – 1830s, memorial portrait, hand-painted, quartz crystal top, rolled gold, 1.4 in. diameter. (Collection of Navon Vance). $650

**Pendant**, mid-Victorian, 1870s – 1880s, St. George and the Dragon, Renaissance Revival, 10 karat gold, en ronde and champlevé enameling, natural ruby, emerald and pearl, pendant, bale and chain is 2.25 in. high. (Author's Collection). Value $1,300

**Pendant**, mid-Victorian, 1860s – 1880s, grape cluster and leaves of carved jet, 2.125 in. high (with bale). (Author's Collection). Value $235

**Photo Locket**, mid-Victorian, 1860s – 1880s, bird in nest of vulcanite, 2.25 in. high. Value $175

**Pendant and Brooch**, mid-Victorian, 1870s, both with floral motif of pietra dura, pendant with bale is 1.75 in. high, Value $300, brooch is 1.625 in wide. (Courtesy of Ebert and Company). Value $195

**Vinaigrette**, mid-Victorian, 1850 -1860, tiger claw, rolled gold, 2.25 in long. (Collection of M.Q. Iacovetti). Value $1,800

Pendant, mid-Victorian, 1860s, cross with foliage of glass and brass, 2.5 in. high 1917 – 1939. (Courtesy of Diana Miller, Out of the Attic). Value $125

Pendant, mid-Victorian, Renaissance Revival, 1870s, marked "Sterling", masque, caryatids, and putti with smokey quartz, 3.375 in. long. (Collection of M.Q. Iacovetti). Value $750

Pendant, mid-Victorian, 1860s – 1870s, tiger claw mounted in rolled-gold (rose), cast yellow gold lion, 1.5 in. long. (Collection of Navon Vance). Value $500

Pendant, mid-Victorian, 1870s - 1880s, Whitby jet cross, gold-filled end-caps with pelleted accents, 1.5 in long. (Courtesy of Roberta Knauer Mullings, G.G.). Value $250

Lavallière, Arts and Crafts, 1900 – 1915, marked "14k", basse-taille enamel, synthetic ruby, natural pearl, 1.75 in. high. (Collection of Navon Vance). Value $185

Pendant, late Victorian, 1880s, Buckle motif of champlevé enamel, 14 karat gold, 1.5 in. high. (Courtesy of Ebert and Company). Value $165

Lavallière, Arts & Crafts, c.1910, marked "14k", diamond, fresh water pearl, gold, 1.75 in. long (with bale) . (Collection of Navon Vance). Value $265

Pendant, Renaissance Revival, marked "14k", 1870 – 1880s, lion, diamond eyes, holding a diamond in his mouth, 0.75 in. high. (Collection of M.Q. Iacovetti). Value $275

**Pendant**, late Victorian, 1880s – 1890s, double-sided pendant has background of butterfly wings, birds made of egret feathers, base metal bezel, 1.75 in. diameter. (Courtesy of Roberta Knauer Mullings, G.G.). Value $175

**Pendant**, late Victorian/Edwardian, 1881 – 1910, roses of celluloid, hand-painted accents and leaves, with ribbon, pendant is 2.25 in. long. (Courtesy of Diana Miller, Out of the Attic). Value $135

**Pendant**, late Victorian, 1880s – c1900, marked "9k", old European cut tourmaline, natural pearl, 1.75 in. high (including bale). (Collection of Navon Vance). Value $245

**Baby Locket**, late Victorian, star motif, faux pearl, rolled gold, 0.4 in. high. (Collection of Navon Vance). Value $55

**Locket**, Art Nouveau, 1890 – 1910, interior photo compartment, gold plated, 2.125 in. long. (Collection of M.Q. Iacovetti). Value $120

**Pendant**, Art Nouveau, 1890 – 1920, flowers 18 karat gold with enameling, 1.5 in. high. (Courtesy of Ebert and Company). Value $1,000

**Pendant**, Art Nouveau, c1900, marked "18k", Plique à jour, 1.25 in. diameter. (Collection of Navon Vance). Value $2,000

**Pendant**, late Victorian, 1880s – c1900, marked "18k", neo-classical revival, female profile, wreath border, 1 in. diameter. (Collection of Navon Vance). Value $175

**Pendant**, Belle Époque, 1910 – 1920, pansy, reverse painted on glass, marcasites, pewter, 1.125 in. high. (Courtesy of Diana Miller, Out of the Attic). Value $75

**Lavallière**, Edwardian/Belle Époque, 1900 – 1815, opal, spinel, and seed pearls set in rose gold, 2 in. long. (Courtesy of Roberta Knauer Mullings, G.G.).Value $525

**Pendant**, Belle Époque, c1900, Edelweiss of carved ivory, 2.25 in. high. (Courtesy of Lisa L. Olson). Value $75

Vinaigrette, Belle Époque, 1900 – 1915, one side with basse-taille enamel, 0.875 in. diameter. (Courtesy of Lisa L. Olson). Value $85

Pendant, Belle Époque, 1900 – 1920, Suffragette jewelry, faux pearl, amethyst and peridot colored glass, rolled gold, 2.25 in. high. (Courtesy of Cristina Romeo). Value $350

Pendant, Belle Époque, Birmingham Hallmarks for 1931, commemorative gold coin minted in 1912 surrounded by small garnets, 1.25 in. diameter. (Collection of Navon Vance). Value $285

**Pendant**, Edwardian, 1907 – c.1920, marked "14k", insignia with two set stones and the words "Qu'hier, Que Demain" (literally translated "than yesterday," "than tomorrow") inspired by Rosemonde Gerard's love poem, possibly made by Alphonse Augis. (Collection of Navon Vance). Value $195

**Pendant**, Art Deco, marked "925", 1917 – 1930, onyx, marcasites, and heart-shaped pastes, 1.5 in. high. (Courtesy of Diana Miller, Out of the Attic). Value $100

**Pendant**, Mid-Century Modern, bolder opal and single cut diamonds, pelleted accents, 18k gold, marked "750", 1.25 in. long. (Courtesy of Roberta Knauer Mullings, G.G.). Value $1,400

**Lavallière**, Belle Époque, 1900 – 1920, marked "10k", shield-shape with laurel wreath, bloodstone, fresh water pearl, gold. (Collection of Navon Vance). Value $150

Pendant, 1950s – 1960s, marked "14k", cottage and foliage set with precious gems, 1.8 in. diameter. (Collection of Navon Vance). Value $340

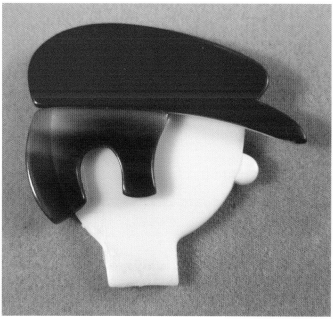

Pendant, Pop Art, 1960s, marked "made in France", portrait of a young man, assembled Casein, 1.125 in. high. (Courtesy of Diana Miller, Out of the Attic). Value $55

Pendant and Neck Chain, Art Nouveau Style, 1960s, central 3.82 ct opal with 16 round diamonds, each 0.06 ct., total weight 22 dwt, marked "Cini" and "14K". (Courtesy of Roberta Knauer Mullings, G.G.). Value $1,600

# Necklaces and Watch Chains

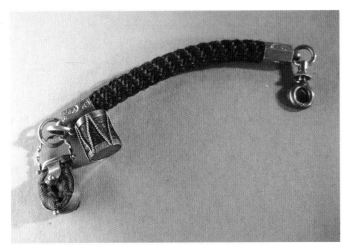

**Watch Chain**, early Victorian, woven hair chain and charms, rolled gold, 4 in. long. Value $125

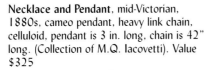

**Necklace and Pendant**, mid-Victorian, 1880s, cameo pendant, heavy link chain, celluloid, pendant is 3 in. long, chain is 42" long. (Collection of M.Q. Iacovetti). Value $325

**Book Chain Necklace**, mid-Victorian, necklace pendant with hard stone cameo, taille d'epargne enameling, rolled gold links, necklace is 17.5 in. long pendant and drop is 2.5 in. long. (Author's Collection). Value $400

**Necklace**, mid-Victorian, 1860s, vulcanite, 19.5 in. long. (Courtesy of Roberta Knauer Mullings, G.G.). Value $250

**Necklace**, mid-Victorian, 1860s, gutta percha, double strand necklace with embossed leaves, rolled gold spacer balls, 18.75 in long. (Courtesy of Roberta Knauer Mullings, G.G.). Value $600

**Necklace with Pendant and Vinaigrette**, mid-Victorian, 1870s, rolled gold and hard stone cameo, reverse with hair and perfume compartments, 20.5 in long. (Courtesy of Roberta Knauer Mullings, G.G.). Value $550

**Necklace**, mid-Victorian, micromosaic, rolled gold, pelleted accents, 18.5 in. long. (Courtesy of Roberta Knauer Mullings, G.G.). Value $500

**Necklace and Pendant**, mid-Victorian, 1860s, horn pendant is 2.75 in. long, glass bead necklace is 49 in. long. (Courtesy of Lisa L. Olson). Value $300

**Necklace**, mid-Victorian, black glass, rose gold, seed pearls, 18.5 in. long. (Courtesy of Roberta Knauer Mullings, G.G.). Value $500

**Necklace**, Arts and Crafts, 1900 – 1915, drop necklace with dark amber colored glass, faux pearls, silver, necklace chain is 16 in. long, pendant is 2.25 in. long. (Collection of Debbie White). Value $100

**Choker**, late Victorian/Edwardian, 1880 – 1910, multi-strand cut-steel, 13 in. long. (Courtesy of finderskeepersvintage.com). Value $250

**Necklace**, late Victorian, 1880s, necklace of hand-made, watch cock-covers, 15.25 in. long. (Collection of Heather Gates). Value $500

**Necklace**, late Victorian, 1880s, necklace of hand-made, watch cock-covers, 15.in. long. (Collection of Heather Gates). Value $500

**Sautoir**, late Victorian, 1880s – 1890s, gray and black beads woven on fabric, 72 in. long. (Collection of M.Q. Iacovetti). Value $350

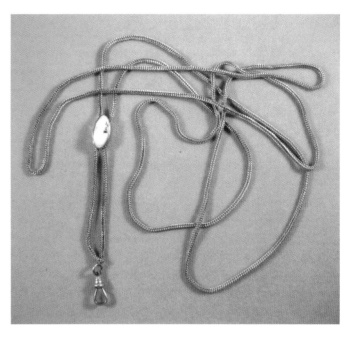

**Slide Necklace**, late Victorian, 1870s – 1880s, small, hard stone cameo slide, rolled gold chain, 47 in. long. (Collection of M.Q. Iacovetti). Value $165

**Sautoir**, late Victorian, 1880s – 1890s, black beads, braided, 84 in. long. (Collection of M.Q. Iacovetti). Value $350

**Necklace/Pendant**, late Victorian, cross of tourmaline-colored paste, neck chain with paste accents, chain is 24 in. long, pendant is 2.5 in. long. (Courtesy of Roberta Knauer Mullings, G.G.). Value $175

Sautoir, late Victorian, c1880, deep orange branch coral, 52" long. (Courtesy of Diana Miller, Out of the Attic). Value $650

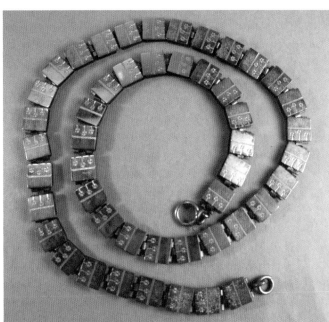

Book Chain Necklace, late Victorian, 1880s, gold filled, stamped design, 18 in long. (Courtesy of Roberta Knauer Mullings, G.G.). Value $250

Watch Chain, late Victorian, seed pearls, gold filled, marked "ASJ Co" 49 in. long. (Courtesy of Roberta Knauer Mullings, G.G.). Value $150

**Choker**, late Victorian/Edwardian, 1880s – 1910, white and black glass beads, 13 in. long, 2.25 in wide. (Courtesy of Lisa L. Olson). Value $300

**Necklace**, late Victorian/Edwardian, 1890 – 1910, marked "Sterling", garland style necklace of crystal and Sterling silver, each individually linked and prong set, 13.5 in. long. (Courtesy of Cristina Romeo) Value $1,100

**Choker**, late Victorian/Edwardian, 1880s – c1910, three strand, central hand-carved rose, ivory, pendant is 1.125 in. high, necklace is 13.25 in. long. (Collection of Navon Vance). Value $400

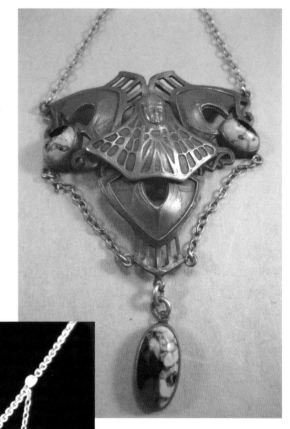

Necklace, Art Nouveau, 1900 – 1915, red and green glass, brass plate over copper, necklace is 14.5 in. long. (Courtesy of Lisa L. Olson). Value $225

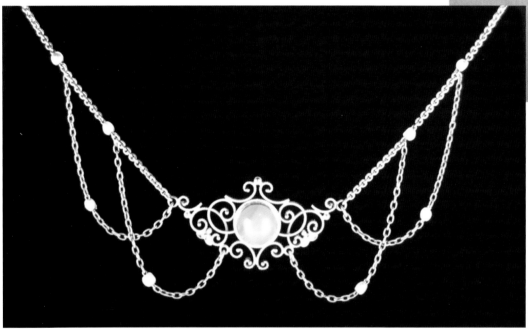

Necklace, Belle Époque, c1900, cabochon turquoise, seed pearls, 14 karat gold, necklace is 14 in. long. (Courtesy of Ebert and Company). Value $1,100

Necklace, Arts & Crafts, calibré cut turquoise, 14 karat gold, pendant is 2.25 in. wide. (Courtesy of Ebert and Company). Value $1,000

**Sautoir**, Belle Époque, 1910 – 1920, multi-colored, butterscotch Bakelite, 60 in. long. (Author's Collection). Value $275

**Sautoir**, Edwardian/Belle Époque, 1900 – 1915, carnival glass beads, 42 in. long. (Collection of M.Q. Iacovetti). Value $295

*Négligée* **Necklace**, Edwardian/Belle Époque, 1900 – 1920s, rose bud pendants of ivory, ivory beads, some discoloration, 34.5 in. long. (Author's Collection). Value $200

**Necklace**, Edwardian/Belle Époque, roses of carved ivory, amber beads in graduated sizes, 25 in. long. (Courtesy of Diana Miller, Out of the Attic). Value $500

Necklace, Art Deco, 1930s – 1940s, blue glass, double linked with garland style, linked small drops, 14.5 in. long. (Collection of Kitty Barrett). Value $375

Choker, Art Deco, 1920s – 1930s, graduated dark orange coral, 10mm to 13mm, 15.75 in. long. (Author's Collection). Value $1,700

Choker, Art Deco, 1917 – 1920s, marked "14K", hollow gold beads, 14" long. (Courtesy of finderskeepersvintage.com). Value $525

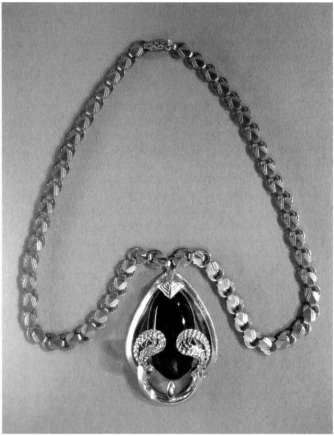

Necklace, Art Deco, 1917 – 1920s, black glass pendant, wide chain embossed with geometric shapes, silver base metal, pendant is 2 in. long, chain is 18 in. long. Value $125

**Necklace**, Art Deco, 1917 – 1920s, geometric shapes in opaque, black and red glass, 18 in. long. Value $125

**Sautoir**, Art Deco, 1917 – 1930s, black, gray, pink and white glass beads, amethyst bead tassel, 32 in. long. (Collection of M.Q. Iacovetti). Value $250

**Necklace**, Art Deco, 1930s, geometric shapes in opaque white glass, 18 in. long. Value $145

**Necklace**, Art Deco, English Hallmarks for 1927, Sterling, 33 in. long. (Collection of M.Q. Iacovetti). Value $650

Sautoir, 1917 – 1925, Art Deco, large, multi-colored glass beads strung with small red glass bead, necklace is 32" long, drop is 5.5 in. long. (Courtesy of Lisa L. Olson). Value $175

Necklace, Belle Époque, 1910 – 1920s, glass, Bakelite and paste, gold filled, pendant is 2.5 in. long, chain is 36 in. long. (Courtesy of Roberta Knauer Mullings, G.G.). Value $165

Necklace, Art Deco, marked "14k" 1917 – 1939, graduated orange coral strand 3mm to 10mm, 17.5 in. long. (Courtesy of Diana Miller, Out of the Attic). Value $300

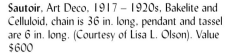

Sautoir, Art Deco, 1917 – 1920s, Bakelite and Celluloid, chain is 36 in. long, pendant and tassel are 6 in. long. (Courtesy of Lisa L. Olson). Value $600

**Necklace and Pendant**, 1920s – 1930s, Geisha Girl pendant and graduated bead necklace, dyed ivory, pendant is 2.75 in. long, necklace is 27 in. long. (Courtesy of Lisa L. Olson). Value $550

**Necklace and Pendant**, Art Deco, Heart-shaped pendant of orange Bakelite, ivory colored celluloid chain, pendant is 2.75 in. high, chain is 25.5 in. long. (Courtesy of Cristina Romeo). Value $1,000

**Necklace**, Asian Art Deco, 1919 – 1920s, carnelian plates mounted with basse-taille and champlevé enameled accents, alternating links of champlevé enameled Chinese characters, brass, 16.25 in. long. (Courtesy of Cristina Romeo). Value $200

**Necklace**, Art Deco, 1917 – 1935, glass pendant, necklace alternates green glass beads with white base metal rose links, 15 in. long. (Courtesy of Cristina Romeo) Value $125

**Necklace**, Arts & Crafts, marked "Czechoslovakia", 1919 – 1920s, opaque pale blue glass, some loss to glass, brass, 14 in. long. (Courtesy of Cristina Romeo). Value $150

**Necklace**, Art Deco, blue glass cubes spaced with brass roundels and glass beads, necklace is 32 in. long, pendant drop is 3.5 in. long. (Courtesy of Cristina Romeo). Value $295

**Necklace and Pendant**, Art Deco, 1917 – 1930s, marked "585", chrysanthemum of carved carnelian, bead accents, gold, pendant is 1.25 in. high, chain is 13 in. long. (Collection of Navon Vance). Value $275

**Necklace**, Art Deco, 1917 – 1930s, Bakelite, graduated single strand, 24 in. long. (Collection of Navon Vance). Value $160

**Necklace**, Art Deco, 1920s, black and ivory glass, leaf-shaped roundels, 18 in. long. (Collection of Debbie White). Value $65

**Sautoir**, Art Deco, 1915 – 1925, multi-colored, round and disc-shaped glass beads, linked in groups of three, 56 in. long. (Collection of Debbie White). Value $275

Necklace, 1920s – 1930s, pattern-molded red glass beads, 50 in. long. (Collection of Debbie White). Value $195

Sautoir, Art Deco, 1930s, amber glass beads, faux pearls, strung on chain, 36 in. long. (Collection of Debbie White). Value $125

Necklace, Art Deco, 1918 – 1935, amber glass and brass, pendant with glass drops, 16.25 in. long. (Collection of Debbie White). Value $175

Choker, 1930s – 1940s, blue glass and composite blue glass beads, brass spacers on chain, 16 in. long. (Collection of Debbie White). Value $85

Necklace, Art Deco, 1918 – 1935, amber glass and brass, 15.5 in. long. (Collection of Debbie White). Value $150

Necklace, 1920s, black celluloid cameo, celluloid beads, brass, necklace is 28 in. long, tassel is 4 in. long. (Collection of Debbie White). Value $85

Necklace, Art Deco, 1930s – 1940s, painted wooden beads, enameled tin clasp, 14 in. long. (Collection of Debbie White). Value $95

Necklace, 1940s – 1950s, graduated cut crystal, silver, 19.25 in. long. (Courtesy of Lisa L. Olson). Value $175

Necklace, Art Deco, marked "Miriam Haskell, 1940s, Lucite orange beads, brass, 24" long. (Collection of Debbie White). Value $230

Necklace, Mid-Century Modern, 1950s – 1960s, triple-strand necklace of red, goldstone glass, red and white crystal, 17.5 in. long. (Courtesy of finderskeepersvintage.com). Value $195

Necklace with Pendant, 1950s, marked "Miriam Haskell", central cabochon with flowers of hematite colored beads, pendant is 3.5 in long, necklace is 20" long. (Collection of M.Q. Iacovetti). Value $165

Necklace, Mid-Century Modern, 1940s – 1950s, marked "Wendell August Forge," daisies of hand-hammered graduated aluminum disks, 18.5 in. long. (Courtesy of Joy Ste. Marie). Value $125

**Necklace and Pendant**, Mid-Century Modern, 1940s – 1950s, marked "Handmade", and "N. Rossi", dogwood flower of hand-hammered aluminum, necklace is 16 in. long, pendant is 4 in. long. (Courtesy of Joy Ste. Marie). Value $95

**Choker**, 1940s – 1950s, glass beads strung and assembled in groups, brass roundels, 17 in. long. (Collection of Debbie White). Value $85

**Necklace**, Mid-Century Modern, 1940s – 1950s, pilgrim collar style, patterned, hand-hammered aluminum, 16 in. long. (Courtesy of Joy Ste. Marie). Value $165

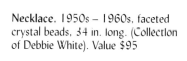

**Necklace**, 1950s – 1960s, faceted crystal beads, 34 in. long. (Collection of Debbie White). Value $95

Necklace, Mid-Century Modern, marked "West Germany", 1945 – 1965, linked, yellow glass beads, 36 in. long. (Collection of Debbie White). Value $70

Necklace, Art Deco, 1930s – 1940s, Lucite and silver-toned beads individually linked, 39 in. long. (Collection of Debbie White). Value $55

Sautoir, Victorian Revival, 1950s, blue glass beads, textured, irridized glass beads, brass, 28 in. long. (Collection of Debbie White). Value $165

Necklace, Victorian Revival, 1945 – 1960s, purple glass, gold-tone plating, 25" long. (Collection of Debbie White). Value $85

Necklace, marked "Goldette", amethyst glass, gold-tone plating, necklace is 18 in. long pendant and drops are 5 in. long. (Collection of Debbie White). Value $75

Necklace, marked "West Germany, 1945 – 1965, black glass, multi-strand necklace with beaded tassels, 28 in. long. (Collection of Debbie White). Value $150

Necklace, marked "Botticelli", silver-tone, 1950s – 1960s, double strand slide necklace, floral motif with tassels, necklace is 23 in. long. (Collection of Debbie White). Value $170

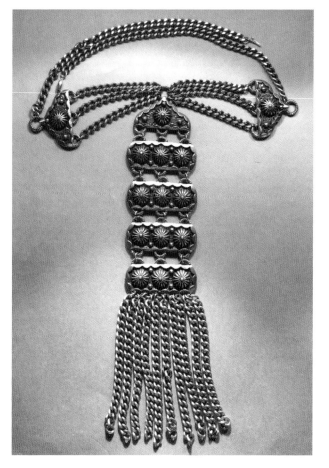

Necklace, Pop Art, marked "Vendome" 1960s, overall length of 21 in. pendant is 7.5 in. long. (Collection of Debbie White). Value $95

## Parurers, Suites, and Sets

**Demi-Parurer**, brooch and earrings, early Victorian, 1840s – 1850s, high relief, lava cameo of Bacchantes, brooch is 2 in. high, Sheppard's hook earrings are 2.25 in. long, original box. (Courtesy of Roberta Knauer Mullings, G.G.). Value $2,800

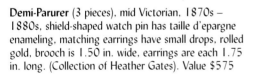

**Demi-Parurer** (3 pieces), mid Victorian, 1870s – 1880s, shield-shaped watch pin has taille d'epargne enameling, matching earrings have small drops, rolled gold, brooch is 1.50 in. wide, earrings are each 1.75 in. long. (Collection of Heather Gates). Value $575

**Parurer**, mid-Victorian, Egyptian Revival, 1860 – 1885, parurer includes three brooches and two pair of earrings of scarab beetles mounted in gold-filled settings, one brooch and one pair of earrings have taille d'epargne accents, largest brooch is 4 in. long. (Courtesy of Roberta Knauer Mullings, G.G.). Value $1,700

**Demi-Parurer**, Brooch and Earrings, mid-Victorian Renaissance Revival, 1870s – 1880s, shield shaped brooch with pendant, matching pendant style earrings, rolled gold, brooch is 2.75 in. long, earrings are 1.75 in. long. (Courtesy of Roberta Knauer Mullings, G.G.). Value $575

**Demi-Parurer**, necklace and brooch, late Victorian, 1880 – c1900, rose-cut garnets and spinel, gold-plated mounting, necklace is 17 in. long, brooch is 1.75 in. diameter. (Courtesy of finderskeepersvintage.com). Value $1,600

**Demi-Parurer**, mid-Victorian, 1870s, Renaissance Revival, rolled gold, brooch is 2.5 in. long, earrings are each 2.25 in. long. (Collection of Barbara Seaman). Value $550

**Demi-Parurer**, brooch and bracelet, late Victorian, 1881 – 1900, sea bean and silver, brooch is 1.75 in. long, bracelet is 7.5 in. long. (Author's Collection). Value $300

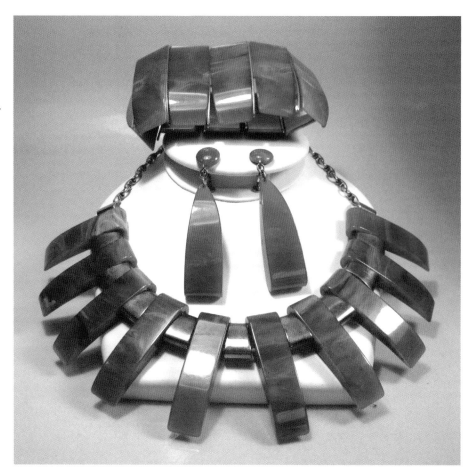

**Suite**, necklace, expandable bracelet, earrings, 1930s – 1940s, Bakelite with brass spacers, necklace is 17 in. long, bracelet is 8 in. long, earrings are each 2.875 in. long. (Collection of Kitty Barrett). Value $1,000

**Suite**, necklace and earrings, Art Deco, 1935 – 1945, gold and silver base metal set with orange glass cabochons and clear pastes, necklace is 18 in long, post earrings are 2 in. long. (Courtesy of Roberta Knauer Mullings, G.G.). Value $600

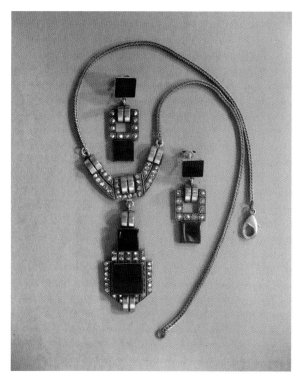

**Suite**, necklace and earrings, Art Deco, 1935 – 1945, gold and silver base metal set with black, orange and clear pastes, necklace is 20 in. long, post earrings are 1.75 in. long. (Courtesy of Roberta Knauer Mullings, G.G.). Value $500

**Suite**, necklace, pendant, earrings, 1930s, roses of ivory, graduated bead necklace, pendant is 1.75 in. high, earrings are each 1.5 in. high. Necklace is 18 in. long. (Courtesy of Lisa L. Olson). Value $520

**Suite**, necklace and bracelet, marked "Czechoslovakia" 1915 – 1925, Art Deco, black and red glass, re-plated, necklace is 22 in. long, pendant is 2.25 in. long, bracelet is 6.75 in long. (Courtesy of Lisa L. Olson). Value $325

**Suite**, bracelet, brooch, earrings, and adjustable ring, Asian export, 1920 - 1940s, dragons of dyed bone, silver filigree mounting, bracelet is 7.875 in. long, brooch is 1.34 in. wide, earrings are each 0.8125 in. high, ring face is 0.875 in. high. (Courtesy of Cristina Romeo). Value $450

**Suite**, necklace and earrings, marked "Hobé", 1930s, black goldstone glass, faux pearls, individually linked brass, necklace is 34 in. long, earrings are 1 in. diameter. (Collection of Debbie White). Value $375

**Suite**, Necklace and earrings, 1940s – 1950s, marked "Sandor", double-strand, necklace has red glass bead, crystal roundel spacers, patterned red glass drops, necklace is 18 in. long, matching earrings are each 2 in. long (Courtesy of finderskeepersvintage.com). Value $300

**Suite**, brooch and earrings, 1940s - 1950s, floral spray with cultured pearls, silver mounting, brooch is 2.5 in. high, earrings are each 0.75 in. high. (Courtesy of finderskeepersvintage.com). Value $275

**Suite**, bracelet and earrings, Matisse, Mid-Century Modern, 1945 – 1965, enameled copper, earrings stamped "Matisse", bracelet is 7.5 in. long, earrings are 1 in. high. (Courtesy of Roberta Knauer Mullings, G.G.). Value $250

**Suite**, brooch and clip-back earrings, 1940s – 1950s, mother of pearl, orange and black glass, brass, wire mounting, brooch is 3 in. long, earrings are each 1.25 in. high. (Collection of Debbie White). Value $145

**Suite**, brooch and earrings, Victorian Revival, 1930s, sterling leaf motif with floral buds, brooch is 3.25 in. long, earrings are 1.25 in. long. (Courtesy of Roberta Knauer Mullings, G.G.). Value $325

**Suite**, brooch and earrings, marked "Balle", 1950s – 1960s, Mid-Century Modern with yellow guilloché enamel, raised Sterling surface, brooch is 2 in. wide, earrings are 0.75 in. high. (Collection of Debbie White). Value $450

**Suite**, fur clip and earrings, marked "Hobé" 1950s, red, white and blue paste, clip is 2.5 in. long, earrings are 1 in. diameter. (Collection of Debbie White). Value $225

**Suite**, two brooches and earrings, marked "David Andersen", 1950s – 1960s, Mid-Century Modern leaf motif, white guilloché enamel on sterling, single leaf brooch is 2.75 in. long, four-leaf brooch is 2.5 in. long earrings are 1.25 in. long. (Collection of Debbie White). Value $600

Suite, bracelet and earrings, Mid-Century Modern, 1940s – 1950s, marked "Napier", tear-drop shapes of beaded base metal, amber pastes, bracelet is 7.75 in. long, clip-back earrings are each 1.25 in. long. (Courtesy of finderskeepersvintage.com). Value $200

Suite, necklace, bracelet, earrings, 1945 – 1960, marked "Trifari", triple-strand necklace and bracelet of white glass and gold-toned beads, large gold-toned earrings with glass drops, necklace is 17 in. long, bracelet is 7 in. long, earrings are each 1.125 in. long. (Courtesy of finderskeepersvintage.com). Value $200

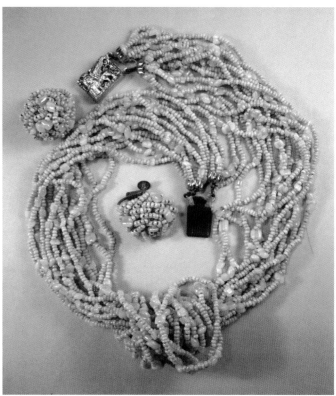

Suite, necklace and earrings, 1950s – 1960s, marked "made in Italy", pale blue, multi-strand, torsade-style necklace 17in. long, knot motif, matching earrings are each 1 in. diameter. (Courtesy of finderskeepersvintage.com). Value $400

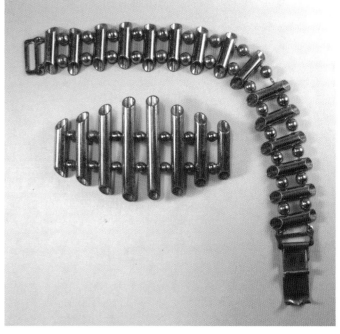

Suite, bracelet and brooch, Mid-Century Modern, alternating pipe and balls, brass, bracelet on chain is 8 in. long, brooch is 3 in. wide. (Courtesy of finderskeepersvintage.com). Value $200

**Suite**, bracelet and brooch, Mid-Century Modern, 1940s – 1950s, both marked "Wendell August Forge", floral motif of hand hammered aluminum, link bracelet is 7 in. long, brooch is 2.125 in wide. (Courtesy of Joy Ste. Marie). Value $145

**Suite**, Necklace and earrings, c1950, marked "Hobé", double strand necklace on chain has double, leaf pendant, matching earrings, light blue and amethyst crystal, necklace is 18 in. long, pendant is 2.25 in. long, earrings are each 1.50 in. long. (Courtesy of finderskeepersvintage.com). Value $600

**Suite**, belt (at left), bracelets (2), earrings, pendant and necklace, Mid-Century Modern, 1940s – 1950s, unmarked, attributed to Wendell August Forge, primroses of hand-hammered aluminum, belt is 46 in. long, link bracelet is 6.5 in. long, cuff bracelet is 2.5 in high, earrings are each 1 in. diameter, pendant is 2.5 in. diameter, necklace is 22 in. long. (Courtesy of Joy Ste. Marie). Value $395

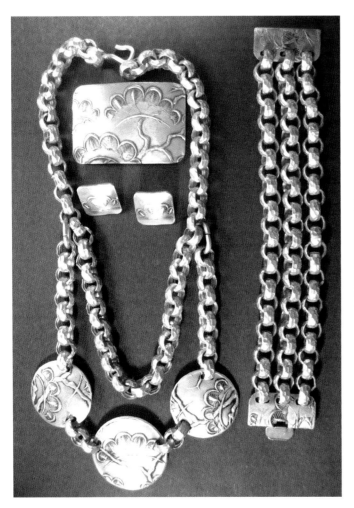

Suite, bracelet, brooch, earrings, necklace, Mid-Century Modern, 1940s – 1950s, necklace and brooch marked "Wendell August Forge", stylized ferns of hand-hammered aluminum, bracelet is 6.5 in. long, brooch is 2 in. wide, earrings are each 0.75 in. wide, necklace is 22 in. long. (Courtesy of Joy Ste. Marie). Value $295

Suite, bracelet, brooch, and earrings, 1950s, white goldstone glass, amber rhinestones, gold-tone base metal, guard chain, bracelet is 7.25 in. long, brooch is 3 in. high, earrings are 1 in. long. (Collection of Debbie White). Value $300

Suite, necklace and earrings, marked "Hobé" black and clear glass, faux pearls, gold-toned base metal, necklace is 16 in. long, earrings are 0.5 in. diameter. (Collection of Debbie White). Value $325

Suite, necklace and bracelet, 1950s – 1960s, gold-toned, multi-strand rope motif, leaf accents, necklace is 15 in. long, bracelet is 7 in. long. (Collection of Debbie White). Value $150

Suite, necklace and earrings, Mid-Century Modern, 1940s – 1950s, Lucite, brass, overall necklace is 24 in. long, pendant is 1.5 in. long, earrings are 1.25 in. long. (Collection of Debbie White). Value $265

Suite, necklace and earrings, 1950s, magenta, teal, and clear glass, double strand necklace, drop earrings, necklace is 28 in. long, earrings are 1.5 in. long. (Collection of Debbie White). Value $200

Suite, necklace and earrings, marked "Art", Asian motif, blue plastic and gold tone plating, necklace chain is 20 in. long, pendants is 4.5 in. long earrings are each 1.5 in. long. (Collection of Debbie White). Value $175

Suite, Necklace, earrings, and bracelet, marked "Hobé", 1950s – 1960s, faux pearls, rhinestone accents, gold-toned base metal with tassels, necklace is 21 in. long, bracelet is 6.5 in. long, earrings are 1.5 in. long. (Collection of Debbie White). Value $350

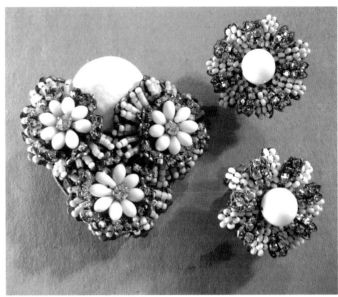

**Suite**, necklace and earrings, Mid-Century Modern, marked "Matisse", 1950s – 1960s, patinated copper, necklace is 36 in. long, earrings are 1 in. high. (Collection of Debbie White). Value $165

**Suite**, necklace, earrings, and brooch, marked "Miriam Haskell", 1945 – 1955, opaque glass beads and rose-cut glass, wired to brass mounting, brooch is 2 in. wide, clip-back earrings are 1 in. diameter. (Collection of Debbie White). Value $500

**Suite**, necklace and earrings, 1950s – 1960s, lavender, amethyst, and green glass, gold-toned, multi-strand necklace with prong-set knot motif, tassels with glass accents, necklace is 24 in. long, pendant with tassels is 4 in. long, earrings are 1.5 in. diameter. (Collection of Debbie White). Value $275

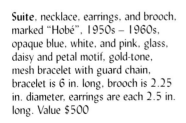

**Suite**, necklace, earrings, and brooch, marked "Hobé", 1950s – 1960s, opaque blue, white, and pink, glass, daisy and petal motif, gold-tone, mesh bracelet with guard chain, bracelet is 6 in. long, brooch is 2.25 in. diameter, earrings are each 2.5 in. long. Value $500

**Suite**, brooch and earrings, marked "DeMario", 1945 – 1960, Mid-Century Modern with faux turquoise and peacock cut crystal, Florentine finish, brooch 2.75 in. long earrings are each 1.5 in. long. (Collection of Debbie White). Value $200

**Suite**, négligée necklace and earrings, 1950s, white glass, silver-toned base metal, necklace is 24 in. long, clip-back earrings are 1.5 in. long. (Collection of Debbie White). Value $375

**Suite**, bracelet and earrings, marked "Matisse" and "Renoir", Mid-Century Modern leaf motif with spotted green enamel, copper, bracelet is 2.75 in. diameter, clip-back earrings are 1.5 in. diameter. (Collection of Debbie White). Value $150

**Suite**, brooch and earrings, marked "Trifari", 1950s, pansies pavé-set with smoke-colored pastes, Florentine finish, brooch is 2 in. diameter, clip-back earrings are 0.75 in. high. (Collection of Debbie White). Value $200

**Suite**, brooch and earrings, 1950s –1960s, leaf motif crystal set in rhodium plating, Florentine finish, brooch is 2.75 in. long, clip-back earrings are each 1 in diameter. (Collection of Debbie White). Value $225

Suite, hinged, bangle bracelet and earrings, 1950s – 1960s, floral buds of amber glass, gold-toned plating, bracelet is 3 in. diameter, clip-back earrings are each 1.625 in. long. (Collection of Debbie White). Value $250

Suite, necklace and earrings, marked "Hattie Carnegie", double-strand necklace of multi-colored and composite glass beads, necklace is 19 in. long clip-back earrings are 1.25 in. diameter. (Collection of Debbie White). Value $325

Suite, necklace and earrings, marked "Hobé", 1950s, multi-strand necklace, gold-tone plating, composite glass with gold flecks, crystal, glass gem-set tassels, necklace is 19 in. long, clcip-back earrings are 3 in. long. (Collection of Debbie White). Value $595

Suite, Brooch and Earrings, c1960, marked "Ming's," dyed ivory and sterling Anthurium flower, brooch is 3 in. long, clip-back earrings are 1.25 in long. (Courtesy of Roberta Knauer Mullings, G.G.). Value $900

**Suite**, two brooches and earrings, Asian, kingfisher feathers, gold plated, floral brooch (top left) is 2.5 in long, butterfly brooch is 1.625 in high, earrings are 1.75 in. long. (Courtesy of Roberta Knauer Mullings, G.G.). Value $1,365

**Suite**, brooch and earrings, marked "Weiss", 1960s, daisies and ladybug, brooch is 2.75 in. diameter, clip-back earrings are 1.25 in. diameter. (Collection of Debbie White). Value $100

**Suite**, necklace and earrings, Mid-Century Modern, gold-tone plating, chain is 17 in. long, pendant is 5 in. long, clip-back earrings are each 1.5 in. long. (Collection of Debbie White). Value $175

**Suite**, necklace and earrings, marked "made in Italy", 1960s, four-strand necklace has foiled enhance blue glass, brass, necklace is 21.5 in. long, clip-back earrings are each 1.25 in. long. (Collection of Debbie White). Value $600

# Rings

Ring, early Victorian, 18 karat gold London Hallmarks for 1854, small mine-cut diamond, natural pearl, champlevé enameled accents, face is 0.625 in. high. (Courtesy of Ebert and Company). Value $800

Ring, early Victorian, buckle motif in rolled gold, buckle lifts to reveal a hair ccompartment, face is 0.25 in. high. (Collection of Heather Gates). Value $250

Ring, mid-Victorian, 1870 – 1885, "Mizpah" of individual charms with champlevé enamel, seed pearls, 18 karat gold face is 0.75 in. high. (Author's Collection). Value $700

Ring, mid-Victorian, 1870 – 1885, marked "C. G." and "18", Etruscan Revival motif with natural pearl, coral, face is 0.25 in. high, 18 karat gold attributed to Carlos Giuliano. (Author's Collection). Value $700

Ring, mid-Victorian, 6.82 carats, amethyst, bezel set, marked "10K", 4.4 dwt. (Courtesy of Roberta Knauer Mullings, G.G.). Value $525

Ring, early Victorian, 1840s – 1850s, mine-cut diamonds, rose gold, face is 0.5 in. long. (Courtesy of Lisa L. Olson). Value $1,300

Ring, mid-Victorian, 1860s, cyma curves and beading, gold plated, band is 0.375 in wide. (Courtesy of Lisa L. Olson). Value $175

Ring, late Victorian, marquise shaped illusion setting with 7 rose-cut diamonds, 14 karat white and yellow gold. (Author's Collection). Value $250

Ring, late Victorian, inscribed "Jan Y 91", top inscribed "MEW", exterior with woven band of hair, rolled gold, face is 0.375 in. high. Value $200

Ring, late Victorian, 1880s, amethyst, yellow gold top, white gold shank with engraving accents, face is 1.375 in. high. (Collection of Heather Gates). Value $500

**Ring**, late Victorian, 1890s, rose-cut, mine-cut, and old European cut diamonds, silver-topped, gold base and shank, face is 1 in. high. (Courtesy of Roberta Knauer Mullings, G.G.). Value $800

**Ring**, Edwardian, c1910, marked "Sterling" black glass cameo, face is 1.125 in. high. (Collection of M.Q. Iacovetti). Value $85

**Ring**, late Victorian, 1880s, Pietra Dura, rose gold, face is 1 in. high. (Courtesy of Lisa L. Olson). Value $375

**Ring**, Belle Époque, 1890 – 1920, shell cameo set with marcasites, sterling silver, 1 in high. (Courtesy of Roberta Knauer Mullings, G.G.). Value $145

**Signet Ring**, late Victorian, 1880s – 1900, phoenix in taille d'epargne enamel, rose gold, face is 0.5 in. long. (Courtesy of Lisa L. Olson). Value $150

**Ring**, Belle Époque, 1900 – 1920, shell cameo, possibly Aphrodite, silver, marked "800". (Courtesy of Roberta Knauer Mullings, G.G.). Value $125

Ring, Edwardian/Belle Époque, 1905 – 1925, Old European cut diamonds, approximately 2.5 cwt (total carat weight) set in 14-karat white gold. (Courtesy of Roberta Knauer Mullings, G.G.). Value $2,000

Ring, Art Deco, 1917 – 1925, marked "835", marcasites set in silver, face is 0.5 in. wide. (Collection of M.Q. Iacovetti). Value $75

Ring, Art Deco, 1919 – 1920s, marked "10k", modern round brilliant (0.33ct), white gold setting. (Courtesy of finderskeepersvintage.com). Value $490

Ring, Art Deco, 1920s, silver and marcasite, marquise-shaped, pierced, replaced shank. (Courtesy of Roberta Knauer Mullings, G.G.). Value $100

Ring, Art Deco, 1917 – 1925, marked "Sterling", rectangular face set with marcasites, face is 1 in. high. (Collection of M.Q. Iacovetti). Value $95

Ring, Art Deco, marked "Sterling", 1917 – 1925, onyx face with initial, face is 0.75 in. high. (Courtesy of Diana Miller, Out of the Attic). Value $125

Ring, marked "14K", 1915 – 1925, Art Deco with amethyst in white gold. (Courtesy of Lisa L. Olson). Value $350

Ring, Art Deco, 1917 – 1925, marked "18k", 0.10ct diamond set in white gold. (Courtesy of Diana Miller, Out of the Attic). Value $275

Ring, Mid-Century Modern, marked "925", 1940s – 1950s, face is 1.5 in. high. (Courtesy of Lisa L. Olson). Value $75

Ring, marked "Siam" and "Sterling", 1940s, blue champlevé enamel, 1 in. high. (Courtesy of Cristina Romeo). Value $45

Ring, Mid-Century Modern, 1940s –1950s, marked "14k", approximately 0.40 cwt (total carat weight) of round brilliant and single cut diamonds set in geometric shapes, white gold setting, face is 1 in. high. (Courtesy of finderskeepersvintage.com). Value $600

Ring, Mid-Century Modern, 1940s - 1950s, marked "800" 14 mm baroque Tahitian pearl. (Collection of M.Q. Iacovetti). Value $500

Ring, Mid-Century Modern, 1950s - 1960s, marked "14k", 4.9 dwt. (pennyweights) face is 1 in. high. (Collection of Navon Vance). Value $340

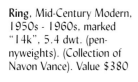

Ring, Mid-Century Modern, 1950s - 1960s, marked "14k", 5.4 dwt. (pennyweights). (Collection of Navon Vance). Value $380

Ring, 1950s – 1960s, marked "14k" rose bud, Florentine and bright polish, face is 0.625 in. high. (Collection of Navon Vance). Value $225

Ring, Pop Art, c1960, Lucite and plastic, top embedded with metal rings, 1.25 in. high. (Courtesy of Roberta Knauer Mullings, G.G.). Value $45

Ring, 1940s – 1950s, rose set with a garnet, 14k, 6.8 dwt. (pennyweights) face is 0.625 in. wide. (Collection of Navon Vance). Value $475

Ring, Pop Art, 1960s, motion ring, moonstones and 14 karat gold, 0.625 in. wide band. (Courtesy of Roberta Knauer Mullings, G.G.). Value $165

# Stick Pins

Stick Pin, Arts & Crafts, 1880s to 1910, abalone blister pearl, silver mounting, gold stem, 2.625 in. long. (Author's Collection). Value $75

Stick Pin, Arts and Crafts, c1900, faux turquoise, faux pearl, gold filled, 3 in. long. (Collection of Navon Vance). Value $50

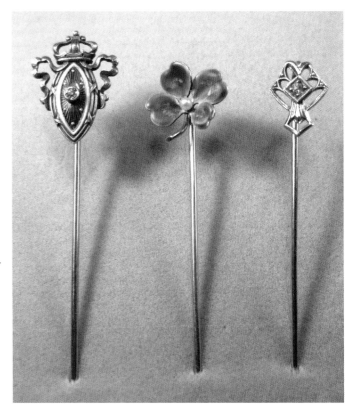

Stick Pins (3) Belle Époque, 1890 – 1915, all marked "14k", from left to right: coronation commemorative with basse-taille enamel and diamond accent, value $125; enameled four leaf clover with seed pearl accent, value $70; Arts & Crafts, white gold pendant with diamond accent. (Courtesy of finderskeepersvintage.com). Value $85

**Stick Pins** (4) Belle Époque, 1900 – 1920, from left to right Mystic Shrine, enameled gold-filled, value $40; enameled chrysanthemum, paste accent, gold-filled value $40; cross with pastes, gold-filled value $45; Arts & Crafts, blue glass, gold-filled. (Courtesy of finderskeepersvintage.com). Value $40

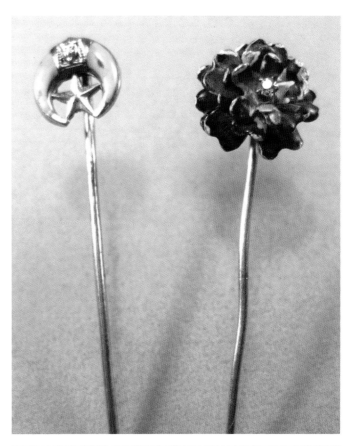

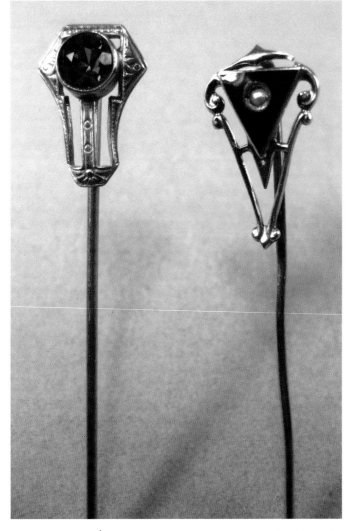

**Stick Pins** (2) Belle Époque, 1900 – 1920, both marked "10k", from left to right: Arts & Crafts with synthetic ruby, value $65; Arts & Crafts with champlevé enamel and seed pear. (Courtesy of finderskeepersvintage.com). Value $50

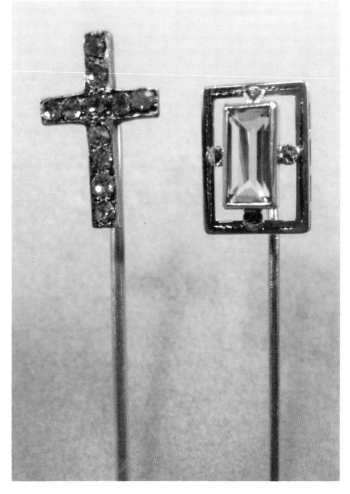

# Watch Pins

Watch Pin, early/mid Victorian, 1860s, seed pearls, white and black taille d'epargne enameling, rolled gold, 1.5 in. long. (Collection of Heather Gates). Value $300

Watch Pin, mid-Victorian, 1870s, branch, knot and tassel, rolled gold, 3 in. long. (Courtesy of finderskeepersvintage.com). Value $450

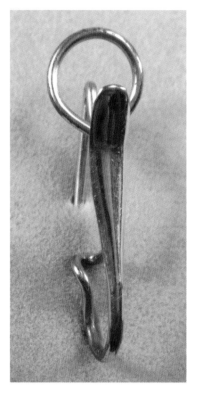

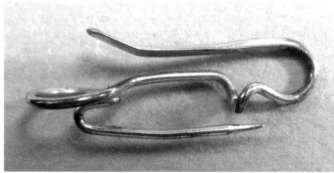

Watch Pin, Arts & Crafts, 1880s – c1900, wire wrap, rolled gold, 1.125 in. long Value $100

Watch Pin, mid-Victorian, gold-filled, shield shaped, hand engraved accents, repaired hinge, 0.75 in long. (Courtesy of Roberta Knauer Mullings, G.G.). Value $125

**Watch Pin**, late Victorian, 1880 – c1900, star motif with cabochon opal, old European and rose-cut diamonds, 0.75 in. long, replaced safety. (Collection of M.Q. Iacovetti). Value $700

**Watch Pin**, Art Nouveau, marked "14k" 1890 – 1917, swans holding cabochon turquoise, 3 old European cut diamonds, 2.25 in. diameter. (Collection of M.Q. Iacovetti). Value $425

**Watch Pin**, late Victorian/Edwardian, marked "800", 1890 – 1910, fleur-de-lis of vermeil, 0.75 in. high. (Collection of M.Q. Iacovetti). Value $110

**Watch Pin**, Art Nouveau, marked "14k", 1890 – 1915, female portrait with flowers, pearl, 1.125 in. wide. (Collection of M.Q. Iacovetti). Value $175

**Watch Pin**, Art Nouveau, 1885 – 1910, marked "14k", flower of champlevé enamel, natural pearl center, 1.0625 in. diameter. (Author's Collection). Value $275

**Watch Pin and Watch**, Mid-Century Modern, 1950s, gold-toned, metal, 7-jewel watch with sub-second hand, overall length is 3.375 in long. (Courtesy of Roberta Knauer Mullings, G.G.). Value $125

# Bibliography

Baird-North Co. *Year Book 1922 Baird-North Co.: The Mail Order House of Quality.* Providence, R.I.: The Co., 1922.

Baird-North Co. *Year Book 1923 Baird-North Co.: The Mail Order House of Quality.* Providence, R.I.: The Co., 1923.

Bell, C. Jeanenne. *Answers to Questions About Old Jewelry, 1840-1950.* Edited by Kris Manty. 6th ed. Iola, WI: Krause Pub., 2003.

Black, J. Anderson. *A History of Jewelry.* New York: Park Lane, 1981.

Bloomingdale's (Firm). *Bloomingdale's Illustrated 1886 Catalog: Fashions, Dry Goods, and Housewares.* New York: Published for Henry Ford Museum & Greenfield Village, Dearborn, MI by Dover Pub. Inc., 1988.

Cassin-Scott, Jack. *The Illustrated Encyclopaedia of Costume and Fashion: From 1066 to the Present.* London: Brockhampton Press, 1998.

Dolan, Maryanne. *Collecting Rhinestone & Colored Stone Jewelry: An Identification & Value Guide.* 3rd ed. Florence, AL: Books Americana, Inc., 1993.

Evans, Joan. *A History of Jewellery, 1100-1870.* New York: Dover, 1989.

Falk, Fritz. *Schmuck-Kunst im Jugendstil: Lalique, Fouquet, Gautrait, Gaillard, Vever, Wolfers, Masriera, von Cranach = Art nouveau jewellery.* Stuttgart: Arnoldsche, 1999.

Farneti Cera, Deanna, and Miriam Haskell. *The Jewels of Miriam Haskell.* Woodbridge Suffolk, U.K.: Antique Collector's Club, 1997.

Farneti Cera, Deanna. *Amazing Gems: An Illustrated Guide to the World's Most Dazzling Costume Jewelry.* New York: H. N. Abrams, Inc., 1997.

Flower, Margaret Cameron Coss. *Jewellery, 1837-1901.* New York: Walker, 1969.

Great Exhibition. *The Art-Journal Illustrated Catalogue of the Industry of All Nations: 1851.* London: G. Virtue, 1851.

James, Ducan. *Antique Jewellery: Its Manufacture, Materials, and Design.* 2nd ed. U.K.: Shire Pub. Ltd., 998.

Jordan, Marsh and Co. *Jordan, Marsh Illustrated Catalog of 1891: An Unabridged Reprint.* Philadelphia: Athenaeum of Philadelphia, 1991.

Markham, Christopher Alexander. *Markham's Hand Book to French Hall Marks on Gold and Silver Plate: Containing 431 Stamps.* London: Reeves and Turner, 1899.

Marshall Field & Co. *1896 Illustrated Catalogue of Jewelry and European Fashions.* Edited by Joseph J. Schroeder, Jr. Chicago: Follett Pub. Co., 1970.

Miller, Judith, John Wainwright, and Graham Rae. *Costume Jewellery.* DK collector's guides. London: Dorling Kindersley Ltd., 2003.

Nadelhoffer, Hans. *Cartier: Jewelers Extraordinary.* New York: H.N. Abrams, Inc., 1984.

National Fish & Wildlife Forensics Laboratory. Ashland, OR, 2008.

New England Jeweler. *Illustrated Jewelry Catalog, 1892.* Mineola, New York: Dover Pub. Inc., 1998.

Newman, Harold. *An Illustrated Dictionary of Jewelry: 2530 Terms Relating to Gemstones, Jewels, Materials, Processes, Styles, Designers and Makers from Antiquity to the Present Day.* London: Thames & Hudson Ltd., 1994.

Percival, Maciver. *Chats an Old Jewellery and Trinkets.* New York: F.A. Stokes Co.

Phillips, Clare. *Jewels and Jewelry.* New York: Watson-Guptill Pub., 2000.

Rainwater, Dorothy T. *American Jewelry Manufacturers.* West Chester, PA: Schiffer Pub. Ltd., 1988.

Rezazadeh, Fred. *Costume Jewelry: A Practical Handbook & Value Guide.* Paducah, KY: Collector Books, 1998.

Romero, Christie. *Warman's Jewelry: A Fully Illustrated Identification and Price Guide to 18th, 19th & 20th Century Fine and Costume Jewelry.* Iola, WI: Krause Pub., 2002.

Sala, George Augustus. *Notes and Sketches of the Paris Exhibiton.* London: Tinsley Brorthers, 1868.

Sanders Cinamon, Diana. *All About Antique Silver with International Hallmarks.* San Bernardino, CA: AAA Pub., 2005.

Scarisbrick, Diana. *Jewellery Source Book.* Rochester: Grange Books, 1998.

Setnik, Linda. *Victorian Costume for Ladies, 1860-1900.* With price guide. Atglen, PA: Schiffer Pub. Ltd., 2000.

Tardy. *International Hallmarks on Silver Collected by Tardy.* 5th ed. English language reprint, 2000.

*The Illustrated Catalogue of the Universal Exhibition Published with the Art Journal.* London: Virtue and Co., London and New York, 1868.

*Trade Marks of the Jewelry and Kindred Trades.* 3rd ed. New York: Jewelers' Circular Pub. Co., 1988.

# Index